That's What Love Is All About

based on the stage play "Who Told You to stop"

LYDIA EUDOVIQUE

ISBN 978-1-0980-5514-1 (paperback)
ISBN 978-1-0980-5515-8 (digital)

Christian Faith Publishing, Inc.
832 Park Avenue
Meadville, PA 16335
www.christianfaithpublishing.com

Printed in the United States of America

Acknowledgments

I give thanks to God who is the head of my life and the giver of all gifts. Without Him, I could not survive the journey that has led me to my destiny. I am thankful for His strength and courage that have kept me through the storms of life. He has showed me that, with Him, I can do all things.

I also thank my Bishop, Demetrius Serieux, who has supported me on this journey and taught me to strive for excellence.

My first lady, Rolda Serieux, who is the president of Omega Sisters Ministry, has taught us all about fulfilling our purpose. I will never forget the day you said to me, "You are such an awesome playwright. Have you ever thought of writing a book?" God used you, First Lady, to plant that seed in me. It took some years, but all in God's time. God bless you both.

To my parents, Joseph and Sheila Eudovique, thanks for raising me up in the fear and admonition of the Lord.

To my three brothers and five sisters, thank you for all your support and encouragement.

To my children, Claudia Leandre, Sharon Alexander, Sherlene Salmon, Marvin Alexander, Marva Belton, and Delvin Alexander you all have been my Pillar of strength.

To my two daughters-in-law—Kathie Alexander and Natasha Alexander—and my sons-in-law—Tchaly, Maurice, and Bryan—thank you all for being a pillar of strength when I needed you.

To all my grandchildren, nieces, and nephews, thank you, thank you, and thank you.

Chapter 1

J oy sat in her living room deep in thought, wondering what she could have done so wrong that would cause her husband Dave to walk away from a marriage of twenty years. She was interrupted by a noise that she did not recognize at first. It was the ringing of her doorbell. *Who could be at my door this hour of the night?* she thought. But before she could answer the door, there was the turning of keys, and she realized that it could only be Dave. He was the only one besides her and their daughter Jazz who had keys to the house. She did not wait for him to open the door but yanked the door open with disgust. "What are you doing here opening my door at this time of the night without even calling first?" she asked.

He pushed past her into the living room before answering her question. "I came to collect the envelope that I forgot here when I came to help you move," he said to Joy.

"I don't know what you're up to, but I've already told you that there is no envelope here. And as a matter of fact, please leave my keys on the table. I don't know why Jazz insisted on giving you the spare keys anyway," Joy responded.

He turned around to leave. Dropping the keys on the table, he said to Joy, "Please tell Jazz that I was here and that I will be picking her up at 6:00 p.m. on Friday." He then walked out the door, slamming it shut behind him.

Joy woke up to the pounding of the rain against her windowpane. She wished she could stay in bed all day, but it was already 9:00 a.m., and Cassie would be coming over in an hour. She had promised Cassie that they would watch the last episode of GH together. While hurrying into the shower, the telephone rang. It was Cassie asking if she could bring Lisa with her. Joy told her it was okay and rushed into the shower. By the time Joy got dressed, Cassie and Lisa arrived, but before they sat down to watch the show, the doorbell rang. It was Dave. He came to pick Jazz up. Jazz said goodbye to her mom and the others and left with her dad. By then, the tension in the room was so tight, Joy knew they were not going to see any show without Cassie saying what was on her mind.

"Okay, Cassie," Joy said. "Out with it. Don't you think I know that you're sitting here about to explode right now?"

Cassie turned to Joy. "Answer me just one question. Why did you give him your address? I thought you said it was a clean break."

"And a clean break it is. Staying in that house was too painful for me, so I moved out. But Dave has a right to know where Jazz is always, and I don't have a problem with him picking her up here."

"What's the difference?" Cassie asked.

"The difference is this is my territory, and he has no say in my life anymore," Joy said.

"And I thought you said he was supposed to pick her up at 6:00 p.m? Oh, so he can just come and go as he pleases?" Cassie continued.

"Listen Cassie," Joy said." I don't have time for this right now, please."

Lisa asked if they could watch the show. Cassie exhaled deeply and decided to drop the subject for now. They watched the show and discussed it a bit. It was after noon by then, and Joy served them up some of her famous casserole. Lisa and Cassie complimented Joy on the meal and wanted to know when she was going to start her catering business. The catering business was something Joy wanted to do for the longest time, but Dave kept coming up with every excuse as to why the timing was not right. Now that she was on her own, she couldn't wait to get started. She shared her ideas with her two friends, and they agreed to help in any way they could. Lisa would be responsible for finding a good location, with Joy's approval of course, and Cassie would take care of business cards and flyers. They discussed the different menus and prices, and the atmosphere was buzzing with excitement by the time they were finished. The one thing they could not agree on was the name of the business. Joy felt that it was her business and it was whatever she chose to call it. However, they were so excited and eager to help that she didn't want to hurt their feelings, and she decided that they should pray about it.

Lisa looked at her watch and realized that it was after 6:00 p.m. She decided to leave because she had to fix dinner for Greg. Cassie wanted to stay a while longer, but since she came with Lisa and would need a ride home, she had to leave also. Both Cassie and Joy looked puzzled. They could not understand why Lisa was in such a hurry when Greg would not be home for the next couple of hours. But talking to Lisa about it now would open a whole can of worms, which Cassie and Joy knew they did not have the time for. They said their goodbyes, and Cassie and Lisa left.

Before Cassie left, she motioned to Joy that she would call her when she got home. Joy knew very much that it was to talk about the situation with Lisa and Greg. For the past six months, there had been some changes in Lisa's behavior. Lisa had missed out on a few book club meetings and did not even call to say she could not attend. Cassie asked her about it, and she gave some flimsy excuses that did not make any sense. Joy noticed that Cassie was taking a while to call so decided to call Cassie.

The phone rang about four or five times, but no one answered. Finally, Joy left a message, praying that all was well. She prayed that God would take care of Cassie wherever she was and cover her and her daughter with His love. Cassie lived alone since her daughter Kaylynn had moved out because of the constant fighting between them. They lived in a not-so-nice neighborhood that was used to crime and violence. She hoped that all was well with Kay, and it was not because of her getting into trouble again that she had not heard from Cassie.

Joy called Lisa. Lisa did not answer the phone, and Joy whispered a prayer for Lisa also. "God, please watch over my friends. I am concerned about them, but I know you have them in your hands. I thank you for your blood that covers them and the anointing that destroys every plan of the enemy against them. I trust you and take you at your word. I stand on every promise that you have made to me. In Jesus's name, amen." Joy slipped under the covers, and as she drifted off to sleep, the telephone rang; it was Cassie. She woke up the next morning wondering if it was a dream, or if she actually did speak with Cassie last night. She tried to recall their conversation and realized that she was not sure, so she decided to call Cassie.

Cassie could not stop laughing when Joy tried to recount the details of their conversation. It was nothing close to the actual thing. However, she remembered they were planning to meet at their favorite restaurant. Joy arrived at the restaurant a bit early and called Lisa while she waited for Cassie. When Cassie arrived, they decided to have lunch outside on the terrace. Cassie ordered her favorite grilled salmon with garlic mashed potatoes and asparagus spears while Joy ordered chicken Caesar salad with a glass of unsweetened iced tea. Cassie settled for water. While they waited for their food to arrive, Cassie told Joy that she was concerned about Lisa.

"I think that idiot has become obsessive. I think he is abusing her, Joy. Ugh, I just want to kick him upside his head."

"I know he is crazy, but I don't think he is that crazy," Joy said. "Actually, I spoke with her just before you got here, and she assured me that everything was okay."

Cassie looked at Joy and rolled her eyes. "And you believe her? I know you know better than that. She hides stuff from us all the time. Remember the time she said she tripped and fell down the stairs?"

"Yes Cas, but if Lisa will not be honest with us, there is nothing we can do," Joy replied.

The waiter arrived with their food, and they ate in silence for a while. Cassie broke the silence by asking the question that had been plaguing her for the longest. "Joy, how do you do it?"

With a puzzled look on her face, Joy asked, "Do what?"

Cassie did not reply right away; she seemed to be deep in thought, and Joy had to snap her fingers to get her friend's attention.

"Cassie, why would you ask me a question and then disappear to God knows where?"

"I'm sorry," Cassie said, laughing. "How could you be so calm and collective all the time? You pray about anything. You trust God for everything. You don't worry or stress about nothing. You make this God thing seem so easy. Even when you found out that Dave was cheating, all you did was pray. Don't you get discouraged or fed up sometimes? I admire you, my friend. Help me understand."

Joy could not believe that she was just sitting here thinking of her friends and how their lives could be so much better if they would surrender to God, and God gave her the perfect opportunity that she was looking for. She told God that she would not bring up the subject with them anymore unless He presented the opportunity. She remembered the last time she tried telling them about His love and grace; it turned into an argument because they felt like she was pushing God down their throat. She had invited them to church many times, and it was one reason after the other why they could not attend. But for the past month, Lisa surprised her twice when she showed up in church without Joy's invitation, and now, here was Cassie's curiosity.

God, you're awesome! Joy used the opportunity to share her experiences with Cassie. "Listen, Cas, an intimate relationship with God is the most precious gift one can possess. You can talk to Him about anything. Even the little things that seems not so important, you can talk to Him about them. It may sound crazy, but one night after Dave left, I felt so alone and lost, I began to cry out to God, and He literally wrapped His arms around me. I honestly felt Him. It's like He just breathed on me, and I fell into the most peaceful sleep I've ever had. But see, Cas, you've got to be real with Him."

"Can I tell you something strange?" Cassie asked with tears in her eyes. "I actually felt His presence when you were talking to me about Him comforting you. I feel such a peace—like I don't have any care in the world. But I'm afraid that I will mess up."

"And whenever you do, God will be right there with arms wide open, ready to turn your mess into miracles," Joy assured her. "Don't let anyone, including the enemy, trick you into condemning yourself because you may slip or even fall sometimes. See, that's the trick of the devil. God is always ready to forgive if you acknowledge your wrongs and ask forgiveness for what you have done."

Cassie did not realize that she was holding her breath until she exhaled long and hard. Joy looked at her friend in amazement.

"What was that all about?"

Cassie smile shyly. "I guess I thought that if I breathed, I would lose the moment, so I just held Him all in. I don't know, Joy." Cassie was laughing harder by now.

Joy looked at her through squinted eyes. "Wow, this is nothing but the joy of the Lord. I love moments like these. I wish Lisa was here with us."

"Me too," Cassie said.

They decided to leave and called for the check. Cassie had taken the train to the restaurant, and since it was getting a bit dark by now, Joy decided to take her home. "I have no one to rush home to, Cas, and Jazz has choir rehearsals tonight. She'll be getting a ride home, so I'm good."

They talked about the possibilities of not hearing from Lisa and prayed for her. By the time Joy dropped Cassie home and got to her house, it was almost eight o'clock. She watched TV for a while and tried calling Lisa again but got no response. She decided to try again in the morning.

Chapter 2

Cassie came home from church feeling very excited about her newfound relationship with God. This newfound joy made the world seem to be a better place. She had called Kaylynn and asked her to come over because she wanted to talk to her. Kaylynn never showed up like she promised to, but Cassie decided that she would talk to God about it and trust Him to take care of it. She could not wait to talk to Joy about the sermon that was preached today. The pastor was talking to her. *Somebody told him all my business,* Cassie thought. *Did Joy talk to him about me? This is too weird.*

Cassie called Joy but got her voicemail. She left an urgent message, hoping Joy would return her call sooner than later. *This is crazy. This can't be real,* Cassie thought. She played the whole sermon over and over in her head. Just when she was thinking about calling Joy again, the phone rang. It was Joy on the other line.

"What seemed to be so urgent that you couldn't wait until tonight?"

They were meeting that night for their monthly book club meeting.

"Please, Joy, tell me that you spoke with the pastor about everything I have shared with you, because that's the only thing that will make sense to me."

"No, girl, why would I do that? Even if it's the pastor, I would never do something like that." Joy was a bit offended; Cassie could hear it in her voice.

"Then explain to me, Joy, how every word that came out of the pastor's mouth was the story of my life."

Joy understood why Cassie would feel that way. "It is the working of the Spirit of God," she told Cassie. "When God speaks like that, it's just to let you know that He sees you and He knows everything that you're going through. He wants you to know that you're not in this alone. He promised that He would never leave you nor forsake you. That's how much He loves you."

Cassie breathed a sigh of relief. "But this can get a bit scary if you don't understand it, Joy."

"I know, but you'll be all right," her friend assured her.

Cassie was silent for a while; Joy asked her if she was all right. She told Joy that she had been trying to reach Kay, but Kay was not returning her calls. Cassie also told Joy that she could not understand why her daughter was so hostile toward her lately. They had a beautiful relationship, and it was like Kay turned into this person that Cassie did not recognize. Her best friend Ayesha got pregnant, and the friends that she had been hanging out with lately were no good. Joy reminded Cassie of the upcoming youth camp.

"I wonder if she'll be interested in going with Jazz?"

"I don't know if she will," Cassie said, shrugging her shoulders. "They used to be so close, but lately, she gets upset when I ask her how come I don't see her and Jazz hanging out anymore."

Joy told Cassie that she would have Jazz invite Kaylynn to summer camp to see if she would be interested in going.

They agreed to meet at Joy's home for the book club meeting at 7:30 p.m. "I hope Lisa comes. I'm worried about her," Cassie voiced her concern.

"Me too," Joy added. "Anyway, see you later. I'm going to get ready for tonight."

"Okay, bye," Cassie said and hung up the phone.

Cassie and Joy had been waiting and hoping that Lisa would show up even if it was almost eight o'clock. She had never been this late before. They were worried because they had been trying to get in touch with her for the past week. They left messages, but she did not respond. They could not discuss the book and decided to reschedule.

"Something just doesn't feel right" Joy said.

"I feel the same way," replied Cassie.

There was a knock at the door. Cassie rushed to open the door and was appalled by what she saw. There was Lisa, with sunglasses and a hat on like she was hoping to hide her identity.

"What in heaven's name is wrong with you? Please tell me that bastard didn't put his hands on you." She pulled the sunglasses off Lisa's eyes. "Why are you wearing sunglasses in the night?" She felt sickened by what she saw. As she pulled her into the house, the light shone on Lisa's face, and that's when Cassie saw the gash on her face and her eyes black and blue and swollen beyond recognition. The old Cassie resurfaced; she gasped in dismay.

"See, that's what I'm talking about. I promise I will go to jail if a man ever put his hands on me. This is some crazy mess."

Joy looked at Cassie and rolled her eyes. She got up, embraced Lisa, and led her to the couch. Ignoring Cassie and her tantrums, Joy was more focused on Lisa's well-being.

Joy turned to Cassie. "I understand how you feel, but right now, we need to be here for Lisa." She turned her attention to Lisa. "What's wrong, Lisa? Who did this to you?" Lisa did not respond.

Cassie looked at Lisa and said, "If you don't answer, I promise I'll call the cops." Cassie picked up the phone and dialed 911. "Officer, I'd like to report a case of domestic violence."

Lisa snatched the phone away from Cassie. "Excuse me, officer, it was a mistake." She turned to Joy and Cassie. "All right, guys. I know you both care about me and I do appreciate it. However, I did not return your call because the situation at home got totally out of hand and I did not want you to get involved. You both were right. He is a jerk. Suddenly, Greg got controlling and very abusive. Yes, he has been abusive before, but it was never physical. Only this time, he happened to answer the phone when the school called me to set up an appointment for orientation, and he went off like dynamite."

"But why was he so angry just because you registered for school?" Joy couldn't understand. But then she remembered her situation. "Some men feel threatened by a strong independent woman."

"I don't understand why. If anything, they should be proud," Cassie said.

Lisa continued to relate the story to her friends. "I found out I was pregnant. Yes, and I couldn't wait to surprise you all at the book club meeting. But that phone call ruined everything."

"Oh, so it's the phone call now?" Cassie asked with disgust. Joy looked at her and urged Lisa to continue.

"I kept saying to him, 'Please, you will hurt the baby,' thinking that was going to stop him. He punched me so hard that I blacked out. The next thing I knew, I was in the ambulance and hurting very badly."

"Who called the ambulance?" Cassie asked.

Lisa continued, "My sister told me that she came to the house after she had been trying to reach me that evening and found me lying on the kitchen floor. By the time I made it to the hospital, I had lost the baby." By that time, Lisa was bawling; her pain was more emotional than physical. "I'm sorry that I didn't tell you guys about the baby. I thought Greg would be happy for us, so I wanted to tell him first."

Cassie and Joy both tried to comfort Lisa. They reassured her that everything would be okay and that they understood. Cassie apologized for her outburst and for misbehaving. "I'm trying to be like Christ, but God help me. Please pray for me. But there's no way in God's green earth, and that's not what the flesh wanted me to say, that I would let anyone take advantage of me again. Oh no, it's not going to happen."

Joy and Lisa looked at Cassie wondering what exactly she was talking about. Cassie saw the puzzled look on their faces, but just ignored it. She realized that it would not be fair to open Pandora's Box if she was not ready to deal with the consequences. She knew her friends would not leave the subject alone until she answered all their questions and she was not ready to deal with it now, but when the time was right, she would. Well, at least that's what she told herself. Joy picked up on it and asked Cassie exactly what she was talking about. She said that she just hated to see men abusing their women and that she would never stand for it. Lisa was nodding off on the couch. Joy asked her to stay the night and let her sister pick her up in the morning. She was very tired and took Joy up on the offer.

"I could use the company, anyway," Joy added.

"What company? By the time you count to twenty, she'll be out like a light and snoring like a horse." Cassie was laughing so hard that Lisa opened her eyes and tried rolling her eyes at her, but they hurt so much because of the swelling that she winced in pain.

"So what am I, chopped liver?" Cassie asked. "How come I don't get the same type of hospitality?"

Joy looked at Cassie and shook her head. "Cassie, would you like to spend the night also?"

Cassie smiled and said, "Not really, I just wanted to know if I had the same privileges as Lisa, that's all."

"What am I going to do with you?" Joy asked.

"Love me just the same." Laughing, Cassie got her things and got ready to leave. She hugged Joy and Lisa and promised to come by in the morning to check up on Lisa.

Joy followed Cassie to the door and was about to lock it when the telephone rang. It was Kaylynn looking for her mom. Joy ran to the elevator to let Cassie know. Cassie asked if she was okay, and Joy said yes. "But she wants to talk to you. She wants to come home."

"Tell Kaylynn that I am on my way home and I will talk to her when I get there."

Joy begged Cassie to take the phone call, but Cassie refused. Cassie walked away. "I will talk to her when I get home. If she can't wait, she can always leave again."

"Cassie," Joy called, but Cassie entered the elevator and closed the door.

Cassie called Joy and apologized for walking away from her. She thought about it while riding home in the cab and felt that she took her anger out on Joy, which was not fair, but Cassie was determined that, no matter what, there was no reason for children to disrespect their parents. Kaylynn was only sixteen years old and paid no bills, couldn't take care of herself, and was still in school. Joy agreed with Cassie; however, she still thought that Cassie should have spoken to Kaylynn when she called.

Cassie did not agree. She felt that if Kaylynn was okay and not in harm's way, then she could wait. She was the one that left home. She did not send her anywhere. She can't always have it her way;

this is not Burger King. Joy realized that they had different opinions on the matter at hand and it was best they agreed to disagree. "I've got her exactly where I want her. She will go to camp with Jazz this weekend or she can return to wherever she came from," Cassie said.

"That's bribery and it's not right. You want her to attend by will, not by force," Joy replied.

Cassie responded with a bit of frustration. "Oh really? Well if it works, that's all that matters. I am tired of this child thinking that she run things in this house. I wonder what happened out there that made her suddenly want to come home? But whatever it is, thank you, God!"

The cab pulled up in front of the duplex where Cassie lived. Nosy Miss Althea was sitting on her porch with Kaylynn. Kay seemed to be crying, and Miss Althea was comforting her. "I just pulled in front of my house, and the neighborhood watchdog is sitting on her porch with Kaylynn, so let me go and deal with this child. This is one more thing for Althea to gossip about. Lord help me, Jesus." They set another date for the book club meeting and said goodbye.

Chapter 3

The camp meeting was a part of the youth ministry designed to develop the social, spiritual, and intellectual skills and growth of the young people. It was a program that took place every summer and was not only for members of the church.

Jazmine was overjoyed when Kay accepted the invitation to the summer camp. They talked about what they were going to wear at each function. Kay asked about the rest of her friends that she had not seen in a long time, and Jazz kept wondering what the reason was behind all this excitement that Kaylynn was displaying suddenly. She decided to wait until the right time to ask. She did not want anything to spoil the moment.

The weekend came and went too fast for Jazz and Kaylynn. They met new friends and reunited with old ones. Believe it or not, they learned a lot about each other that surprised them both.

"Could you imagine that after being friends since kindergarten, I am just finding out that your favorite color is brown?" Jazz asked Kaylynn.

Kaylynn replied, "And could you imagine that, after all this time, I am just finding out that you don't like milk? So tell me, friend, what did you do with the milk I used to give you with the cookies when you would come over to my house?"

Laughing hysterically, Jazz could not even catch her breath. "I was hoping that you would never ask. To be honest with you, I used to give it to the cat when you were not looking. I am so sorry."

"You're sorry, all right. All you had to do was tell me," Kay said, smiling. "You're a mess. You know, Jazz, I can't believe that it's been a week already since we got back from camp. On another note, I want to thank you for inviting me to the Youth Summer Camp (YSC) last weekend. I'm glad I said yes. It brought back so many memories. I honestly missed you and all my friends at church."

"You're welcome, but what made you stop coming to church?" Jazz asked. "You stopped taking my calls. Even when I would leave messages, you wouldn't return any of them. I came by your home one day and I knocked on the door, but you would not let me in. I knew you were in there because I could see you through the window. You knew that I saw you. It hurt so much, why?"

Kaylynn looked at her friend with tears in her eyes. "We were together the whole YSC weekend, and you never asked. Why now, when everything seems so perfect?"

"I didn't want to bring it up because I did not want to take away from what the weekend was all about," Jazz said, "but masking your feelings will not take care of the situation. I know there is a root to all your problems, but if you don't face them head on and deal with whatever they are, it doesn't mean that they will go away. Look, Kay, if you don't feel like talking right now, I understand. But whenever you want to talk, just know that I'm only a phone call away," Jazz reassured her.

"I thank God for you, Jazz. The apple really doesn't fall far from the tree. You're just like your mom. The day you and Aunty Joy walked into our lives was the best thing that happened to us. Thanks for being there and for being so understanding. You are the only one that I feel safe with to discuss what has been going on with me, but are you sure you're ready for this?" Kay asked. Her eyes glistened with tears as she looked at Jazz with grief.

Jazz hugged her and felt the hot tears rolling down her shoulder. "Listen, Kay, with the help of God, we can do this."

Jazz held Kay's hands and listened intently as Kay opened her heart to her. "I found out something that my mom never told me, and I wished she had. It hurt so badly because the person who told me didn't mean me any good. Why didn't she tell me? I resent the fact that I had to hear it from other people. I was at my grandma's, and we had an argument and she blurted it out. You can only imagine the impact it had on me. I was shocked, hurt, insulted, and angry all at the same time. I stopped going to church because I started to drink and smoke to numb the pain. I wanted to lay down and die. Sometimes I would pretend that it was a dream and that I would wake up to reality, but that was my reality, and I had to face it every day."

"Oh, Kaylynn, I'm so sorry. I wish I could do something to make the pain go away." Jazz comforted her friend. "But let me ask you a question. How are you so sure that what you heard is true? It could just be some gossip that people are spreading."

"Well, I always felt like Grandma didn't like me. She just tolerated me," Kay explained. "It's strange, but I never understood why she would find fault with everything I did. It's like I could never do anything right for her. You should have seen the look on her face when she insulted me. It was a look of disgust—like she couldn't stand me. She was waiting for the perfect time to hurt me. Jazz, I begged my Mom to come home because, lately, I've been feeling sick, and I'm afraid that I could be pregnant."

Once Kaylynn started to talk, she could not stop. But the one thing that Jazz could not get pass was the possibility of Kay being pregnant at sixteen. She hardly heard anything else that Kay said to her. It was a lot to take in, but she had to compose herself in order to be there for her friend. Jazz took a deep breath and asked Kaylynn the question that was taunting her.

"What was it that your grandma said to you?" But before Kay could answer Jazz, Joy and Cassie came home. Cassie said good afternoon to Jazz and Kay, but Kay did not respond to Cassie. She only responded when Joy greeted her.

Joy was appalled by Kaylynn's behavior. She told Kay that her behavior to her mom would not be tolerated, especially when she was around. "I don't care what happens between you and Cassie, you need to remember at all times that she is your mother and you need to respect her."

Kay's anger reached a boiling point, and it was obvious in her response. "Respect her, Aunty Joy? Really? She is my mother, but ask her who my father is? Go ahead, Aunty, ask her. Maybe she will tell you the truth. Tell her, Mom. You have done nothing but lie to me. Every time I ask, you tell me something different. When I was two, you told me that he was dead. Then let me see, when I was around six, you told me that you didn't know where he was. When I was ten, you told me he was in the military. Which one is the truth, Mom? Oh yeah, you conveniently left out the fact that you slept with your father!"

Crying hysterically, Kaylynn collapsed on the floor. Jazz took Kay into her bedroom as Cassie started to cry and begged Kay to give her a chance to explain. Kay did not want to talk to her mother, so she went into the bedroom with Jazz.

Joy could not understand what had happened, so she decided to give Cassie a chance to pull herself together. "Cas, listen to me, whatever is going on, you all need to fix this and fix it soon. This is crazy. There is too much hostility and hurt between you and your daughter. My advice to you is that you don't wait any longer. I don't know the details, but from what I gather, it's not good. So now that you have calmed down, I'm going to call Kay because you all need to talk. Do you need some privacy or would you rather have Jazz and I there? It's your choice."

"No, I prefer to have you both here with me;" Cassie said. "I need all the support I can get right now."

Joy called Kay and encouraged her to give her mom an opportunity to explain the whole situation. Kay was hesitant at first, not trusting that her mom would be honest this time, but she finally gave in.

Cassie apologized to Kay for not telling her the truth. "Every time I decided to tell you, I would get so scared. I'm not making any excuses for the way I handled the situation. I'm just asking that you understand."

"Oh, so this is all about you now?" Kay said with frustration.

Cassie hesitated for a while, wondering if it was worth it. Maybe she should not even bother. But Joy looked at her and nodded, giving her the support she needed to continue. "On my tenth birthday, your grandma went to work, and after work, she stopped by the bakery to pick up a birthday cake for me. Dad left the house and came back with a gift in his hands, and I knew it was for me. He said, 'here, baby girl, just what you've always wanted. Go ahead, open it up.' I opened up the beautiful red velvet box that Dad handed me, and inside was the most beautiful gold bracelet with my name engraved on it.

"I hugged him tight and said, 'Thanks, Dad, you are the best dad in the world.'

"Dad looked at me and said, 'Come inside, I have something else for you.' I hurriedly followed him as he led me to the bedroom, and he began to tell me that he had been watching me grow up into a beautiful young lady and he loved me and wanted to show me how much, but it had to be our secret. I looked at him with a puzzled frown because, for some reason, I began to feel uncomfortable. He began to touch me in places that he had no business touching. I pushed him away, but he got forceful with me and put his hands over my mouth to muffle the screams as he had his way with me. The pain was unbearable that, for a moment, I blacked out.

"All I remembered afterward was being in the shower and trying to wash the dirty feeling away. I was scrubbing so hard that my skin hurt. When Mom came home, he acted as though everything was normal. A couple of my friends came over to celebrate with me. They sang happy birthday, and I was smiling so hard I thought my face would crack. All the while, I was trying to keep the tears from falling. I could not eat anything. I tried to eat a piece of cake, but just the thought of it made me sick to my stomach. All I wanted was for the party to be over so I could go to my room and hide under my covers. As the last one of my friends left, the tears started rolling down my cheeks. I rushed into the arms of my mom as I said to her, 'Why did he do it, Mom? He hurt me. Why did he hurt me?' I explained to my mom what happened. She hugged me so tight like she was apologizing for what he did to me, but she did not answer my question. She did not answer. She just told me go to bed and that everything would be all right.

"Every time I tried to talk about it, she would change the subject. The abuse continued until I got pregnant with you at the age of fifteen. After you were born, the fights were constant, so Dad left, and we never saw him again. At that time, the gap between us was so wide that it seemed irreparable. It was like she hated me. I felt like she was blaming me for it. Kay, that's why I hesitated to tell you. This is not easy, and I did not know how you would handle it." She turned to hug Kaylynn, but Kaylynn pulled away from her.

"Why didn't you tell me, Mom? You should have told me. After all the different stories you told me, to think that I had to hear the truth from someone else." Kay asked to be excused and went into Jazz's room.

Joy suggested that they spend the night with her and Jazz, but by the time she ordered pizza and went in to call Kay and Jazz, they were fast asleep. Cassie decided to turn in; she was exhausted and needed some rest. Joy watched TV for a while, and as she put the rest of the pizza away and turned off the lights, she whispered to God, "Dear God, I know you will fix this too. Heal the hearts of Kaylynn and Cassie. Mend their relationship, and let them have a personal encounter with you. Put Your love in their hearts that they will forgive each other, for Your perfect love casts away all fears. In Jesus's name, amen."

Chapter 4

Jazz came home from church still basking in the anointing. She was hoping her mom would hurry so that they could leave to deliver the food for the engagement party but, most of all, to talk about the way God moved in the service today. She could not stop thinking about the young lady who sat in front of her. For some reason, she felt the urge to reach out to her from the day she visited. Jazz had been watching her and promised that the next time she came to church, she would. There was something that made Jazz feel like she had seen her before, but she just could not put her finger on it.

Just when she was deep in thought, Joy walked into the kitchen. She asked, "Jazz, why didn't you wake me up?"

Jazz was still thinking about everything that happened at church today and did not hear her. Joy wondered what was going on with Jazz and shook her lightly.

"What's going on with you, young lady? You are a million miles away."

Jazz spun around to face her mom. "Mom, I did not even hear you come into the kitchen. How long have you been standing there?"

Joy responded with a puzzled look on her face. "Long enough to call you twice, and you seemed to be so deep in thought that you did not hear me."

Jazz discussed the events of the morning service with her mom, asking her advice on how to approach Janelle. Janelle was the name of the mysterious young lady, her mom informed her. Joy also told Jazz that she felt like she knew Janelle from somewhere.

"See, Mom, I know I'm not crazy. I know that I've seen her before. I just can't remember where and when. But I promise you, I'll remember."

"If you just relax and stop trying so hard to remember, when you least expect, it will all come back," Joy said. "Come on, let's hurry. The engagement party is at 8:00 p.m., and it's 6:40 p.m. We have an hour and twenty minutes to get there and set up."

Joy and Jazz loaded everything in the van. They checked the list to make sure they did not forget anything. As they pulled out of the driveway, Jazz called Kaylynn to make sure she was still coming. She assured them she was already on her way and would be there by the time they got there.

Kay was very excited to work with Joy in her catering business. Although it was only part time, she felt important and good about herself. She was always on time, and even when things got busy and she had to work an extra day or two, she was always happy to say yes.

The relationship between Kay and her mom had somewhat been strained. They spoke only when necessary, and Kay decided to stay to herself. She would be in her room most of the time and would only come out to eat and do her chores. Cassie demanded that she not eat in the room. Cassie had gotten the two-bedroom apartment that she had applied for, but it was a sacrifice to maintain the bills by herself, and Kay knew that. The extra days she would work was to help her mom with the bills. She made life as easy as possible for her mom. She would do the laundry, cook, and keep the house clean.

Dinner was ready whenever Cassie came home. Sitting at the table was very uncomfortable since conversation was not something they participated in, so Kay would always cook early so she could eat by herself. She told Jazmine that she felt sorry for the ordeal her mom had to go through as a young child.

"No child should be victimized like that," she said. She had so many questions that she wanted to ask her mom, but she could not stand to see her mom hurt the way she did when she had to relate the whole sordid story the other day. How to bring up the conversation was her dilemma. The bus came to her stop, and as she got out, she saw Jazz and Aunty Joy pulling up. Thank God she reached just in time. She hated being late.

They went about setting up things and got ready to serve since this was part of the agreement. Joy didn't serve at functions; she just delivered the food, but since the client begged her to and because the servers cancelled at the last minute, she agreed. It was a beautiful setting, and Kay fantasized about her day. Would it ever happen for her, she wondered. Joy had to snap her fingers to get Kay out of her daydreaming state.

"Come on, child. Remember, you're on the clock. Or maybe I should dock your pay for the couple minutes you stood there staring into space."

"Sorry, Aunty Joy. Just got a bit carried away," Kay said, still smiling.

As the evening progressed, Joy realized that God had set her up just so He could show up. The guests started asking for her business cards, and by the end of the evening, she was able to book five events—two for next week and three for the week after. She updated her calendar and had to shuffle somethings around, but she was so excited that it didn't even matter. Heavenly Taste, as she called her business, was her pride and joy, and right now, she was in heaven.

She told the girls about the name that God gave her for her catering business, and they loved it. For now, Joy worked from home, but with the way things were moving, she knew she would have to find a place soon. Lisa oversaw that, but since the ordeal with her and Greg, things had slowed down a bit. She had booked two locations for Joy to check out the following day, and they all decided to go with her.

By the end of the month, Joy had enough bookings for the next three months to keep her very busy. Lisa and Cassie agreed to help as much as they can, and Jazz agreed to put more time in. For some reason, Lisa felt an urge of excitement as she helped Joy with the business. It gave her a push and determination to go back to school and finish what she started. She had never called the school back to find out the date of orientation since the altercation with Greg, but looking at Joy now and how God was blessing her, she knew what needed to be done. Sitting there just thinking about it, she thought to herself, *It's early. Maybe they're still open*, and she made the call.

Lying in bed that night, Lisa could not believe that her whole life was about to change with one phone call. Fortunately, she called right on time. There was a class starting next week, and orientation was tomorrow. She was faced with two choices—either she could take some of the classes online or at the south campus, which was an hour's drive. She had learned that the north campus, which was right across from her, was not offering fashion design anymore, but she could still take most of her prerequisites there. Lisa was on a high and was not going to let anything get in her way this time. She called the girls, and they decided to meet at their favorite place for lunch the following day. Orientation was at 10:00 a.m. and would be over around 12:00 noon, so they scheduled lunch for 1:00 p.m., that way they could all go with Joy after lunch to see the spaces and decide.

As they sat down to lunch, they were filled with anticipation. Lisa decided to include them in her decision making. First, she shared with them the information that she learned about the fashion design program. She left the part about the location and the two choices that she was faced with for last. They all were very excited for her but realized that there was a problem.

"What's the matter?" Cassie asked.

"Oh, nothing. It just seems like nothing good comes easy. But this time, I am determined that nothing is going to stop me—or no one, as a matter of fact. I have a decision to make, and I need your help in doing so."

Lisa explained that the interior design program was no longer offered at the campus nearby, it was only offered at the south campus, which was an hour's drive. They advised her to take her prerequisites online and then she could get an apartment close to the south campus when it was time to start the program.

"But I'm going to miss you all so much. You are my family."

"You have to do what's best for you. Follow your dreams and pursue your passion. We want you to be the successful businesswoman that we know you are. As much as we will miss you, we understand," Joy said.

"We do," Cassie added. "I can't believe that I'm actually going to miss you, but it will be worth it. You'll see. I wish I had the courage to step out and do something with myself."

"And why can't you?" Lisa asked.

"The thing is that I don't know what I want to do," Cassie replied.

"Pray about it" Joy said.

"Yes, I know. I pray about everything, but if it works for me, it can work for you too."

Just as Cassie was about to respond, the waitress came to take their order. The rest of the afternoon went by with laughter and fun as they enjoyed their meal. They said their goodbyes and promised to meet for dinner at Joy's house on Sunday.

Chapter 5

Joy had been begging Jazz to be her business partner, but Jazz insisted that fashion was her passion. Aunty Lisa had promised her an intern position at her boutique whenever she was ready. Lisa graduated top student in her class, she had receive a scholarship to attend one of the top fashion design schools. She worked part time in a boutique close to the campus while she finished her studies, but her plans were to return home and open her own boutique. She also started her own clothing line, which was doing very well and was already in some department stores. Jazz thought about the sketches she had already started and could not wait to show Aunty Lisa. She was excited because Lisa had called and asked her to be her assistant in managing the boutique. This would mean giving up her current job and getting transportation.

Jazz was eager to hear from her dad about the car that he promised her. It would be much easier for her to go to school and work, and her mom would not have to always schedule her appointments around her. "Mom, do you think Dad will keep his promise and fix the car for me?" she asked.

Joy tried her best not to speak bad about Greg to Jazz, so she chose her answer very carefully. "Only God knows, my child, but ask him. You never know."

"I know you, Mom. You don't think he will, huh? I have nothing to lose, so I'll ask him. I know that he has not done anything that he has promised lately, but I need that car. Besides, Aunty Lisa will be coming home soon, and I'll be helping at her boutique twice a week until I resign from my job. If Dad messes up this time, he has no one to blame but himself."

There was a knock on the door, and both Joy and Jazz admitted that they were not expecting anyone. Joy opened the door only to see Lisa standing there. They did not expect her for another week or so. They both hugged her at the same time. "What are you doing here Aunty Lisa?" Jazz asked. "I mean we did not expect you until next week." "Well I am here, and I am hungry, after a whole hour of driving I could eat a cow." Jazz informed her that they were about to have lunch and would be happy if she would join them.

As soon as they sat down to eat, Cassie called to say she was coming over and to please save a plate for her. Joy fixed a plate for Cassie and one for Kay, knowing that Kay would kill her if she knew that they had Aunty Joy's casserole because of course her mom would mention it. Everyone knew Cassie could not keep a secret.

Cassie arrived sooner than later and was surprised to find out that Lisa was in town and no one had bothered to mention it to her. "So this is what is going on behind my back? How come y'all having a party without me?" Cassie asked.

No one answered because they were not going to fuel that fire. "Girl, come on in. We just wanted to surprise you, that's all," Joy said.

Lisa explained to her that she was not suppose to return so soon, but since she did not have to take the finals, she was able to come home sooner. As usual, Cassie found something slick to say. Kaylynn arrived soon after, and they all agreed that this would be the best time to watch the movie that Lisa brought with her.

Jazmine and Kaylynn knew better; they knew that once those three got together, they would be more talking about what was going on with them than watching the movie. Quietly, they excused themselves and went to Jazz's room to "catch up on things."

As soon as the girls left, Joy, Cassie, and Lisa began "catching up on things." Cassie wanted to know all about the opening of the boutique and how she could help. "I did a pretty good job helping Joy if I may say so myself. You know it's true, so let's be honest."

Laughing Lisa said, "Yes, you did, you surely did. I saw the pictures. I think you have a knack for something more than always cussing people out."

Rolling her eyes at Lisa, Cassie said, "I don't do those things anymore, missy. I'm not saying that I'm perfect, cause some folks will try you, but I'm trying, right, Joy?"

"Yes, you are," Joy said, "and it will get easier with time and prayer. But you know, I admired the way you decorated my office. Like Lisa said, you do have a knack for it. I like the décor, and how you selected the furniture, so don't think it went unnoticed. I think it's something you should follow up on."

Cassie couldn't help laughing out loud. She did not say anything to her friends, but since then, she had also helped her neighbor with the decorations for her daughter's bridal shower and had gotten compliments about it. She had been seriously thinking about going to school for event planning and interior design, especially since Mrs. Collins, who had the beauty salon next door, had complimented her on it. She had to have done an awesome job because that lady was mean as a Rottweiler and didn't give compliments to anyone.

"Come back to us, Cassie, from wherever you wandered off to," Lisa said, looking at her strangely.

"Are you okay?" Joy asked.

"Yes, I am," Cassie replied. "I've been thinking about interior design or event planning for some time now but have not made up my mind. The thing is though, I really enjoyed myself when I was doing it. It gave me some sense of accomplishment, and at the same time, made me feel kind of giddy like a kid in a candy store. It was fun. I really enjoyed it. But then her thoughts were interrupted by the face of Donovan Taylor flashing across her mind"

"What is it that you really enjoyed? Because you're somewhere out there, I'm not sure where, but you're definitely not here with us." Cassie shook her head as if to recompose her thoughts as she replied, "Um…yeah, yeah, I'm good. I'm here." They all started to laugh, wondering what was going on with Cassie. She had never been tongue tied before or at a loss for words. Cassie looked at them and was about to explain, but she decided that she would just let it go; she knew her friends were watching her keenly, and she was not about to go down a road that made her feel more lost than she already did.

Minister Taylor at her church seemed to be occupying her thoughts lately. *Where is Cassie?* she thought. *I'm losing myself.*

Cassie told them that she would call the school to get information on the interior design and event planning courses and then take it from there. They were all excited and told her how proud they were of her. The girls came out of the room and Kaylynn asked, "So, Aunty Joy, how was the movie?"

Joy said, "Ask Aunty Lisa. It was all her fault."

"Don't pay her any mind, Kay. Then if that's the case, I'll be leaving so I won't be blamed for anything else. No, but it's getting late and I'm tired. I just got back and need to get some things straightened out before bed tonight, but, Jazz, I'll come by tomorrow so we can start working on plans for the boutique." Lisa wished them all a good night and left.

Cassie and Kay decided to stay a while longer. The relationship between them had gotten much better, but they still had some ways to go. Cassie was concerned that Kay might be pregnant. Her friend Aisha had just given birth to a baby boy, and they had been hanging around since the fight between Kaylynn and her mom. Kaylynn had lost a whole lot of weight, and her mom was really concerned. She complained of headaches and nausea all the time, and she always had a runny nose. Cassie decided to take her to the doctor and was awaiting the results of the blood test, but every day that went by, she got more nervous.

The following day, Lisa stopped by like she promised Jazz she would do. Cassie and Kaylynn also came by to help Lisa plan for the opening of the boutique. As they were finishing up, Cassie got a phone call and explained to the rest that she had to leave with Kay because the call was from the doctor's office, asking them to come in right away.

They waited for what seemed like forever. "What is taking Cassie and Kay so long?" Lisa asked Joy. But Joy seemed to be in her own world and did not respond. She was praying for her friend and her daughter. She did not like how she was feeling in her spirit. *Oh my God, what if Kay is pregnant*, she thought. *What is Cassie going to do? Being a single mom, she is in no position to help Kay take care of a child.* She had talked to Kay about giving the baby up for adoption if she was pregnant, but Kay was dead set against it.

Lisa tried to pray. Something was wrong. It had been four hours since Kay and Cassie left. She tried calling but got no answer. It was getting dark, and she had to go, but Lisa didn't want to leave Joy alone; as a matter of fact, she did promise that she would wait here until Kay and Cassie return.

Just when Lisa was trying to decide if she should leave, someone knocked at the door. *Lord, please let that be them,* she prayed silently. Joy opened the door. It was the UPS guy who was delivering a package for her. Joy did not even look at the package; she just threw it on the table and sat down on the couch. Lisa came and sat beside her as they held hands and prayed together.

Jazz came out of her room and sat on the couch besides Aunty Lisa and her mom. Her eyes were swollen from crying. Kay had not long ago expressed her fear of being pregnant to Jazz, and Jazz had assured her that everything would be okay. *It's probably just a bug or something,* she said, but as Jazz thought about it, it brought her no consolation. For some reason or another, she felt something was wrong. Jazz rested her head on her mom's shoulder and felt a sense of peace. Mom hugged her tightly and then reached out and held Lisa's hand when the phone rang. It was Cassie calling to say that they were on their way.

Cassie and Kaylynn finally returned from the doctor's office, but the looks on their faces were not good. Everyone was holding their breath, waiting to hear what they had to say. They were standing around, and Joy asked if they would please take a seat.

"Well, guys, Kay is not pregnant, but oh how I wish that she was instead of what else I have to say. The result shows that she is HIV positive."

The room seemed to spin, and Jazz had to hold on to her mom to steady herself. They all gasped at the same time as they came to terms with the reality of what they just heard. There were no words; everyone was numbed. Cassie asked if they could spend the night. She could not bear the thought of being alone with Kay tonight. If she was distraught, she could only imagine how Kay felt. She did not know how she would feel by tomorrow, but right now, she needed to lie down. "I don't know if I will be able to sleep tonight. God, please help me." She had cried so much that she had a headache.

Lisa hugged Kay and Cassie and got ready to leave. No one was saying much; they all seemed to be in shock. Lisa said that she was leaving and would be back in the morning. Joy locked the door after Lisa left and decided to make some coffee for the three of them. Kay said that she did not want anything and retired for the night. They drank their coffee, not saying much while trying to watch the program that was playing on the television. After a while, Jazz also decided to go to bed and said goodnight to Auntie Cassie and her mom. Joy and Cassie sat staring at the TV, not seeing nor hearing anything that was on. They finally gave up and went to bed.

Chapter 6

It had been two weeks since Kay's visit from the doctor's office. Sitting here at Joy's house with the rest of the family, Kay had something to say and asked for their attention.

"Aunty Joy, Aunty Lisa, Mom, and Jazz, I thank you all very much for your love and support. These past two weeks have given me a lot to think about. When I got the news of my diagnosis, I felt numb and in shock for the first hour. Then I went into denial, depression, anger and, finally, the blame game. However, I have learned a lesson of what true love is all about. You have stood by me even when I was being difficult and tried to push everyone away. And, God, You love me so much that when I wanted to take my life and just end it all, You gave me a reason to live." Kay broke down and began to sob.

Cassie rushed to her daughter's side and began to comfort her like only a mother could. It had been a long time since the others had seen them behave like mother and daughter. By this time, they were all crying. Cassie wiped her daughter's eyes as she said, "I wish it was me. After we left the doctor's office, we walked around for hours on the beach until it began to get dark. We talked to God and were determined that we were not going to leave until we got an answer. God is so awesome that He answered all our questions although it was not what we expected in the way that we expected it. So many things made sense then. I got to hug my daughter and tell her how much I love her. Oh it felt so good to hold her in my arms and just let her cry until she was satisfied. But hearing her say I love you to me was the most precious gift I could ever ask for. I knew at that time how much God loves me. His love united me and my Kay in a way that only He can."

"I have a testimony," Kay said. "You know, I'm beginning to understand purpose. I asked God to make me understand the reason why I'm going through this. Don't get me wrong. I know there are repercussions for the choices we make in life. I know what I did. But what are His plans for me in this mess? Deep inside, I heard Him say, 'My child, there is someone out there that needs to hear your story. I'm not done with you as yet, for in all of this, I will show my glory through you.' Hallelujah! Oh come on, somebody, I feel like preaching. I am talking to all the young people out there—and even the older ones too. I'm not saying what I did was right, but what the enemy meant for bad, God is turning around for good. Look what one night of pleasure got me. I was looking for love and thought I could get it in the arms of men, but the love of God is what I needed. I also learned the lesson of forgiveness. I was able to forgive my mom, and this has brought us closer than we were before. I forgive the man that fathered me. I don't know him, but I have come to know God and the peace of God that passes all understanding. Nothing else matters. I just want to live for Him."

By then, the presence of God was all over the place, and Lisa could not keep still. When she shouted, it came from way deep down inside. "The joy of the Lord is my strength," Lisa said. "This is so amazing to see how the love of God has transformed our lives. I can see the mighty hand of God moving in my situation. I too understand purpose. God loves me. Even with me losing my baby, He was directing my life and ordering my steps. I was able to go back to school and start up my own business. I too can encourage others to pursue their passion and live their dreams. God can turn your trials into triumph, your mess into miracles, and change you from a victim into a victor. I am so empowered that I want to go down the streets and say to everyone I meet, 'Look at me! Look what the Lord has done.'"

"Amen!" Joy shouted. "A lot of people may not understand why we are giving God praise, but having a personal relationship with God is the most precious thing one can possess. During all our circumstances, God is there. Look how He made Himself known to Kaylynn and Cassie. When you have a personal encounter with God, you can never be the same again. When I look back over the years and see how God has kept me, I know He will do the same for you and your mom, Kay. And, Jazz, I have something to tell you. I received the official divorce papers in the mail yesterday. I was going to tell you before everyone came over."

Jazz came and hugged her mom. "We will be okay, Mom. I know. God will never leave us nor forsake us. He has kept us this far. This is just another phase of the journey. He is a faithful God, and I know He will do what He says He will do. I am not discouraged nor sad. His purpose will be accomplished. It's not about us, but it's all about Him. I am just the follower. He is the leader. All I know is that God is a miracle worker." Jazz added. "I don't know where to start and what to say. I have been praying for my best friend for the past six months. I was so happy when she accepted the invitation to camp. I knew that was a start, and I trusted God to finish what He started—and what a transformation."

Lisa was sobbing uncontrollably. She looked at Cassie and said, "The love of God is truly amazing. I never thought I would be able to feel such love for you. It can only be God. I used to tolerate you before wondering how Joy dealt with you. But I can truly say I love you so much and thank God for you. I guess I couldn't deal with you telling me the truth."

Laughing, they all came together in a group hug.

"I don't know where we will be next year around this time," Lisa continued. "We all have started a new journey in life and have learned so many lessons. We will be going into the new year soon, and I trust God that this time next year, we will have greater testimonies to share."

"I have one now," Kay said. "I will be working with the YCC, volunteering on weekends. I am so happy for the opportunity to work with young people. See, that's answered prayers. Mom, I thank God for you. You could have turned your back on me because I did not make it easy for you. That's why I will encourage the young people to obey their parents and to love and respect them. We don't always know what's best for us. Trust me, I used to think so. Now I realize how wrong I was, and which is true, Mother knows best. Come the beginning of the new year, I will be starting, so please, y'all, pray that God's purpose will be fulfilled in my life."

They all gathered at Joy's on New Year's Eve, looking back at the last year and thanking God for where He has them. Kay was looking forward to working with the youth at the YCC program while assisting Aunty Joy at Heavenly Taste Catering. However, she also wanted to pursue her PhD in psychology. Cassie had registered for classes in interior design starting in January. Jazz was so excited to be working in the boutique with Aunty Lisa. She showed her sketches to Aunty Lisa and was very excited that Aunty Lisa would help her with the sewing. Heavenly Taste Catering would be opening another location soon. While they were all catching up on things and wishing each other God's blessing in the upcoming year, the fireworks started, and they realized it was the new year. They hugged and cried and held hands while they prayed, thanking God for His love and blessings. They had agreed to spend the night at Joy's house.

"I can't believe I'm sharing a room with you, Cassie," Lisa said. She was surprised by Cassie's response.

"That's what love is all about."

Chapter 7

Lisa could not believe time had gone by so quickly. She never thought she would be here today five years later standing in her own boutique and having boutiques at other locations. She was a businesswoman, an entrepreneur, and a woman of excellence who loved the Lord. Sometimes, she thought of the child she had lost. Would she be where she was today had things gone differently? Greg had gone to jail for domestic violence and manslaughter for the death of their unborn child. She heard that he was a model citizen in prison and that his lawyer was trying to have him released earlier for good behavior. Sometimes, she found herself feeling a bit antsy knowing that he could be out any day. She just wished with all her heart that he would spend the entire eight years in jail. However, she had to trust God, for He makes no mistake.

Jazz was in the back unpacking some boxes when Lisa called her to come to the front so that she could use the restroom. Standing at the register, the telephone rang, but before Jazz could answer it, a customer walked in the boutique. At first, Jazz had to close her eyes and open them again to make sure she was seeing right. There, standing in front of her, was none other than Greg.

Immediately, she was seething with anger. She thought she had forgiven this man, but she could not just stand there; she had to exhibit the same customer service that she would with anyone else. She came from behind the counter and greeted him. "Uncle Greg, is that you?"

"Girl, you know it's me. Come here and give me a hug. My, how you have grown into a fine young woman." As he released her, his hands sort of lingered somewhat over her body, making her feel a bit uncomfortable. "Where is Aunty Lisa?" he asked Jazz, looking at her as if he was assessing her from head to toe.

"She is not here. Can I take a message?" Jazz replied.

"Yes, please ask her to call me. Don't forget, because I have a meeting tomorrow, and I will be leaving for Chicago the following day," he said.

"Can I have your number?" Jazz asked.

"My number has not changed. And, Jazz, please don't forget."

As he left the boutique, Jazz swore he winked at her. *Oh god, am I hallucinating?* She just remembered that she did not answer the phone earlier and hoped it was not a customer. Just then, the phone rang again. She could hardly concentrate and had to take some deep breaths to settle her nerves before answering the phone. Thank God it was Kaylynn.

"Girl, what is wrong with y'all down there? Is everything okay?" Kay asked, but without waiting for an answer, she continued to tell Jazz that she heard Greg was released last week and she just wanted to tell Aunty Lisa to be careful. Jazz thanked her but did not tell her what had happened. All Jazz needed was for Kay to tell Aunty Cassie, and we all know what would happen."

Lisa returned to the front of the boutique, holding her chest. She overheard the conversation between Greg and Jazz "I thought I was going to have a heart attack." She said to Jazz.

Jazz hugged her, pulling a chair for her to sit. "Let me get you some water." Jazz went in the back to get a bottle of water from the tiny refrigerator that Joy had given Lisa when she opened the boutique. In the meantime, Lisa closed her eyes and prayed to God for His peace. As Jazz returned with the water, Lisa told her that only a couple of days ago, Cassie and Joy asked her what she would do if Greg came around and tried to talk to her.

"Yes, Aunty Lisa. What would you do if you were standing out here when he walked through that door and tried to talk to you?"

Lisa replied sadly, "You know, I never thought about it. But since I heard about his early release, I've been a bit nervous. There is no telling with this man. For instance, there is a restraining order against him. He is not to be within a certain perimeter of me, but guess what? He still showed up here. How did he know where the boutique was anyway?"

"Hmm, that's a good question. I hope it's not through Aunty Cassie. You know his mom has been bothering Aunty Cassie with questions about you, right?"

Lisa looked at her. "Are you serious, Jazz? Not Cassie. Cassie can't stand the ground that woman walks on and blames her for always making excuses for Greg. She wouldn't give her or her son the time of the day. And what does that woman want with me anyway? She never had anything good to say about me. She would say stuff like, 'Oh, Greg could have done better, you're not his type,' and anytime I asked her to talk to her son, she would always find a way to blame me for everything that went wrong in our marriage"

Lisa and Jazz were so deep in conversation that they did not see Cassie walk in.

"What seems to be so interesting that y'all didn't hear me come in? Is that how you do business, Miss Lisa?" Cassie asked.

Jazz did not give Lisa a chance to respond. "No, Aunty Cassy, Uncle Greg—"

But Lisa interrupted Jazz before she could finish what she was about to say. "Hey, Cassie. It's good to see you. How are you?" She was hoping that Cassie did not notice that she had cut Jazz off.

Cassie decided to humor them, so she played along. "I'm good. I like what you did with the place. Wow, I'm impressed. So how are you and how is business?"

"I'm great, and business is booming. All I can say is that God is good Cas," Lisa responded.

"And my eyes are good too," Cassie continued. "Y'all think y'all slick. You really think I didn't see when you interrupted Jazz? Come on, out with it. What's really going on here? You're nervous and fidgeting like a fish out of water."

Taking a deep breath, Lisa thought she might as well. Knowing how Cassie was, she wouldn't let it go, and even if she did not answer her, within the next hour, Joy would be calling because Cassie would call her.

Lisa gave Cassie an account of the whole sordid story. She admitted to her that hearing Greg's voice also brought back a lot of memories. It left her a bit rattled, nervous, and confused. Cassie couldn't understand why Lisa would be confused. "I understand a bit rattled and nervous, but confused? Okay, Lisa, please explain to me again. What is there to be confused about?"

Lisa was trying hard to put her thoughts together so her friend would understand. "I know this may sound crazy, Cas, but hearing Greg's voice had my emotions all over the place."

Cassie looked at Lisa, wondering if her friend had lost her mind. "Do I need to remind you of the abuse that you suffered at the hands of that man? Look, I am trying not to revert to the old Cassie, but you're not making it easy for me. He beat you mercilessly until you lost the baby, Lisa. I don't understand you and half the women in this world that don't believe that they deserve better."

"Listen, Cassie, I know that I deserve better, but I'm not ashamed to admit that I still have feelings for him. My feelings for him will not just disappear overnight. We were married for seven years."

At this time, Cassie had reached her boiling point. "And he abused you for five of those years. Do I need to read your resume to you? Okay, I can't argue with the fact that you still have feelings for him. I don't understand it because he spent five years in jail, but it is what it is. However, you need to put those feelings under subjection."

Lisa turned to Cassie. 'Look, you have never been married, so you won't understand commitment and loyalty. I stood before God and man and took those vows and meant every word of it, so walking away is not as easy as you're making it sound."

Jazz stood there motionless, wondering what had taken a hold of Aunty Lisa. Knowing how Aunty Cassie could get, she could not leave her and Aunty Lisa alone, but she felt sick to her stomach and could not believe what she was hearing. She remembered Uncle Greg hugging her and how she felt. She excused herself and decided to take her lunch now; she just needed to get away.

"Wait a minute," Cassie said. "I may have never been married, but the man that comes my way will have to love me like Christ loves the church. And as for those vows, they need to rewrite them. What is the meaning of for better or for worse and for richer or for poorer? Obviously, some twisted version of the truth."

"And what is truth, Cassie? Uh, please tell me since you know so much for someone who has never been married."

Cassie looked Lisa dead in the face, refusing to feel hurt by her outburst. She thought that she and Lisa had come a long way. All she wanted was for her friend to know her value and not feel that she must settle. Cassie felt that Lisa had hit her below the belt, and she didn't know if they could get past this one. However, she wanted to let Lisa know that because of God's love, she knew that she was not going to accept nothing but the best.

"Look, Lisa, I know what true love is. God loves me unconditionally. Love is patient, kind, and merciful. Love is giving of one's self. Love doesn't hurt. Love is sacrifice. Love protects. That's what love is all about."

Cassie left the boutique knowing that if they don't pray for Lisa, she would find herself in a whole lot of trouble once again.

Chapter 8

Lisa and Cassie usually met at Joy's house for their monthly book club meeting. Joy asked them to come for 6:00 p.m. instead of 7:00 p.m. to discuss the book and still have dinner before it's too late. Cassie arrived first and was waiting for Lisa. She was hungry and asked Joy if they could eat first since they had not heard from Lisa and was not sure if she was coming anyway. They usually ate after discussing the book, but the last time they decided to eat first, everyone got sleepy, and the book was never discussed. Cassie insisted that they eat first since there were interesting matters to discuss tonight instead of the book.

"What interesting matters are you talking about, Cassie? I'm tired of the fussing and fighting all the time. Looking back over the years, it was always something. I thought we were all grown up and decided to do better by letting people walk their own journey. I know it's hard sometimes, and we want what's best for each other, but some people must burn to learn. Look at me. Not tonight, you understand me? No drama! And besides, I thought you and Lisa were best friends now. You help out at the boutique sometimes, and she is helping you with your school registration and stuff. What happened?"

"Why are you jumping all over me? You don't even know what I'm talking about," Cassie replied.

Joy apologized. "I'm sorry, Cassie. You're right. I shouldn't jump to conclusion. Is it Jazz?"

"No, it's not Jazz. Jazz thinks she's grown and knows everything. It's not like I'm asking her to marry Ja'vaughn. Just go out with him."

Ja'Vaughn was a young man who had been pursuing Jazz for some time now, but she wouldn't give him the time of day.

"I know you have Jazmine's best interest at heart, Cas, but she has told you time and time again that she is not interested in Ja'Vaughn and has no intention of going out with him, so could you just please leave it alone?" Joy tried to emphasize this in a friendly manner so she wouldn't offend Cassie, but Cassie was determined to convince Joy that if Jazz only give Ja'Vaughn a chance, she would see that it is worth it. However, she did not want this to cause a problem between herself and Joy, so she decided to drop it.

"Well, Joy, I will not say another word to Jazz about Ja'Vaughn. It's her loss."

"Yeah right, we'll see," Joy replied with a sense of humor. "By the way, how is Kay doing?" she asked Cassie.

"She is doing great. She is determined to get that degree no matter what. I missed her so much. I never thought I would see the day we would get so close. Can you believe it's been five years already since she graduated and went off to college? I truly thank God for giving us a second chance."

Joy responded with such excitement. "He is an amazing God, and I am proud of her for being so determined. I can't wait to see her this weekend. Cassie, she is still coming home this weekend, right?"

"I hate to disappoint you, Joy, but she decided that she would stay and take some extra classes so that she can graduate a semester earlier," Cassie informed her.

"Well, she has to do what's best for her. Although I'm really going to miss her, I do understand. How is her friend, Cas? I still can't believe she gave him the time of day. Remember the sad letters she used to write to you, feeling like no one would ever love her enough to marry her because of her situation, you know, being HIV positive."

"I know, but, Joy, why do you keep referring to him as her friend? His name is David. Not every David is as crazy as that Dave you were married to."

Joy gave Cassie a there-you-go-again look. "All right, maybe I'll just call him D for short."

"And Kay will kill you. That's her pet name for him, so put on your big girl panties and get over it, Joy."

They continued in conversation as they waited for Lisa, wondering if she was ever going to show up. She had been very scarce lately. Cassie told Joy of the event that took place at the boutique last week when Greg came looking for Lisa. They both were concerned that Lisa might get herself in trouble again.

"See, when it comes to that man, Lisa acts like she has no sense, and that's why she hides stuff from us," Cassie voiced her concern to Joy.

Joy shook her head. "I just don't understand," Joy responded. "You would think with all the beatings and losing the baby that she would come to her senses. The fact that she didn't mention the boutique episode to me means that she has something to hide."

"You think?" Cassie replied.

"I wonder if she knows the meaning of the word truth."

"We'll find out today if she shows up," Joy said.

"No, you'll find out today, and that's if she shows up," Cassie continued, "because when I stopped by the boutique the same day Greg was there, Jazz started to tell me what had just happened, and Lisa conveniently interrupted her, pretending that she was so glad to see me. Girl, she jumped on me as though we were long lost cousins or something."

Joy laughed, shaking her head.

"Listen, Joy, let's hope we get the truth out of her today once and for all," Cassie said. "The truth and nothing but the truth, because she told me some story the other day that had so many holes in it, so good luck with that."

But before Joy could respond, the doorbell rang. Joy turned to Cassie. "Remember what I said. No drama!"

Lisa greeted Joy and sat down at the table. She was very hungry and asked if they could eat first and then discuss the book later. But since that was also Cassie's request and Joy said no, Cassie watched Joy with the evil eye to see if she would now let Lisa have her way.

Cassie cleared her throat and looked at Lisa. "I know I'm not invisible."

Lisa replied while rolling her eyes at Cassie. "Hi, Cassie, it's so good to see you."

Cassie, being who she is, said, "I'm sure. Joy, I hope you're not going to change the order of things now."

"Well, since I'm outvoted, we might as well," Joy replied just to aggravate Cassie. She knew that wasn't going to sit well with Cassie, and of course, Cassie took the bait.

"Oh no, no, no, no. You said no because the last time we did that, we all got sleepy and we did not discuss the book anymore. That's what you said."

Joy stood with her hands on her his hips and looked Cassie dead in her face. "And I also said no drama! Since this is my house, I get to have the last say."

Cassie looked at Joy, wondering if she was serious, but before she could ask the question, Joy broke the ice by saying that she was just kidding, but they could compromise by eating while they discussed the book.

They began to share their life stories with each other, and soon, the book was forgotten. Cassie had a story to share with the others that would blow their mind. She was nervous and didn't know what to do. She needed their advice, so she told all, holding nothing back. Minister Donovan Taylor, director of the music ministry at church, seemed to be taking quite an interest in her. They all gasped at the same time, because Cassie seemed to be tickled by this for some strange reason. Knowing Cassie, it was hard for them to believe that she was sitting here acting like a teenager experiencing her first crush.

"How long has this been going on?" Joy asked.

"About two months ago," Cassie replied.

"Go ahead, I'll deal with you later," Joy added.

Cassie continued to explain to them how this all came about, stating that he sent her his phone number by his sister Angela, who didn't seem to like Cassie very much and thought that her brother could do better.

"She actually said that?" Lisa asked.

"Yes. She said that he is wasting his time trying to talk to somebody like me. Girl, I wanted to reach out and slap her right across her ugly face."

Joy reminded Cassie that her relationship with God was personal and that, no matter how much Angela got on her nerves, it was no excuse for her behavior. "I know it's hard sometimes. I'm not going to sit here and pretend that it's easy, but you can do all things through Christ who strengthens you."

They were very happy for Cassie and encouraged her to pray about it. "We will be praying also, but whenever you need a listening ear, we'll always be here for you, right, Lisa?" Lisa agreed.

Cassie thanked her friends and breathed a sigh of relief. "Now it's your turn, Joy" Cassie said.

Seeing that Lisa was sitting next to Cassie, Joy wanted to know why Cassie had conveniently skipped Lisa and came to her, but Cassie, always being Cassie and always starting trouble, said to Joy, "I just want to save the best for last. Besides, I don't want to spoil my appetite."

Joy decided to go ahead and update her friends on what had been happening lately.

"Well, as you know, Dave continued to harass me about some mysterious papers that he left over here. Jazz and I have turned this house upside down looking for the envelope that he claims he left here but can't seem to find it anywhere."

"I think that man wants you back, but he is too full of pride to admit it," Cassie added.

"And why would you think that when he was the one that kept telling me that I should put my business on hold? Every time I would try to launch the business, he would come up with one excuse after another as to why the time is not right. Wouldn't he still feel threatened now that my business is up and doing so well?" Joy continued.

"Some people never miss the water until the well runs dry, and I think he misses you like crazy because he finally realized what he had," Lisa added.

"Well, if what you say is true, God will really have to help him," Joy said. "So he better start praying from now on and stop bothering me, because this business that God has blessed me with isn't going anywhere. I don't mind treating my husband like a king, but I better be his queen, and that's all I'm going to say on this matter."

Lisa shared with them the situation at the boutique when Greg came by. The girls found it hard to believe that she did not know he was coming. However, Lisa explained to them that he had been trying to reach her through his mom, Meddlesome Mattie, as she was known. His mom tried to convince Lisa that if she gave him another chance to work on their marriage, she would see that he was a changed person. Lisa decided to give him the opportunity to hear what he had to say, but it would have to be done over the phone. She did not trust him and decided it was best. As usual, he manipulated her into meeting with him by telling her that she could choose the place and time if that would make her happy, and she gladly did because she felt like it gave her control over the situation.

The girls were furious with her, which made her feel like she couldn't do anything right where her friends were concerned. Lisa thought they would be proud of her this time because she had control over when and where she would meet with Greg, but what she did not realize, it was just another ploy for Greg getting his own way, because in the end, he still won.

"Do you still love him?" Cassie asked Lisa.

Lisa took a while to respond but admitted that she didn't know for sure, but one thing she knew was that the day he came to the boutique and asked for her, feelings began to resurface. "I was nervous, yes, but something happened to me emotionally that I just can't explain."

Joy consoled Lisa by telling her it was okay to feel how she felt. "Listen, Lisa you don't need to be ashamed of your feelings for Greg. I understand that your feelings will not just disappear overnight... Well, in this case, over the years. However, don't let your emotions control your decision. You must think with a clear head. You have been married to Greg for seven years and made history together. It's okay if you still love him, but don't let this be the deciding factor. We may be a bit overprotective, but it's not like we don't have reason to be. Remember the beatings and how he kicked that baby right out of you. All we want is for you to be careful, and please don't listen to his momma, child. You are a praying woman. Get into your prayer closet and talk to God. He hears and answers. But keep us updated, and we will also be praying. Right, Cassie?"

Cassie did not respond but rolled her big eyes at Joy.

Lisa turned to Cassie. "See, this is the same reason why I did not say anything. Can I speak freely and not be judged? I know you want what's best for me, and I appreciate that, but at the end of the day, I am a grown woman, and it's my decision to make."

"Well, well, well, I guess she told you, Miss Joy," Cassie responded, but Lisa decided that she was done and had nothing else to say. Cassie then decided that she had one more thing to say to Lisa before she left. "Lisa, no one is judging you. You are one of those people that must burn to learn. But you know that we love you, that's all. Listen, it's getting late, and I've got to go, but before I go, Lisa, please be careful. I don't trust that man. I never did. There is just something uneasy about him. I can't seem to put my finger on it, but I know what I feel. At least promise that you won't go anywhere with him at nighttime."

Joy agreed that Cassie was right and asked Lisa to call and update them on the meeting with Greg. Lisa assured them that she would pick the place and time and that she would update them as soon as the meeting was over. Joy hugged them as they said their goodbyes and promised them that she would call them the following day with another appointment for the book club.

Chapter 9

The girls gathered together at Joy's house for a welcome-home dinner that she had prepared for Kaylynn. Kay had graduated with her PhD in psychology and intended to open her new office here in downtown Atlanta. She was offered a top paying job in California, where she attended graduate school, but her heart was at home. She thought of all the people who couldn't afford treatment and counseling and wanted to help them by offering free therapy and counseling at her clinic. If Dr. Laundry did not agree to see her even when her mom could not afford the payments, she would not be here today. It was the scholarships she had received that had helped put her through school. All she wanted to do was give back to her community.

The dinner was awesome, and Joy baked Kay's favorite pineapple upside-down cake for dessert. They could not have enough, and Joy told them that it would be okay to take some home. They complimented Joy on her cooking, which caused her to look at her daughter sideways.

"We're not going down that road again, Mom. I've told you time and time again that fashion is my passion," Jazz said.

"I can hope, can't I?"

Jazz responded, "I'll always help whenever you need me, you know that."

Joy decided to drop the conversation and focus her attention on the reason why they were there. Which was to celebrate Kay.

Kay realized that David had left them for a while and wondered what was taking him so long in the bathroom. She began to feel a bit frustrated and went to check on him. As soon as she attempted to knock on the bathroom door, she overheard him talking to someone on the phone. That made her feel a bit more frustrated. *Why would he be on the phone so long*, she thought to herself, *and who was he talking to?*

David came out to join them and sat down on the couch close to Kay. He felt her body stiffened up and asked her if she was all right. Kay asked him what he was doing in the bathroom that took so long because she overheard him talking on the phone. Everyone looked at her in surprise because she was angry and did not bother to hide it.

David tried his best to keep his composure as he replied, "Kay, I was talking to my mom on the phone, and, honey, we have already decided that we would not do this anymore. We have to trust each other, remember?"

"Yeah, I know. I'm sorry I don't know what came over me," she said. She reached out to hug him as she apologized to him.

However, David did not hug her back but said to her, "Look, I've worked so hard to get you. Do you think I'm going to mess this up? I'll be stepping out a bit, but I'll be right back." He then hugged her as he left with Lisa, Cassie, and Jazz, who were going to the boutique to relieve the young lady who worked part time and to close the boutique.

As soon as David left, Joy called Kay to sit by her on the couch because seeing what just happened between her and David was a cause for concern.

"Do you really love this man?" Joy asked her.

"Yes, Auntie, I really do," Kay responded with much enthusiasm.

"And has he given you any reason whatsoever to doubt him?" Joy continued to question her.

"None whatsoever. Every time I think I'm over the mistrust and doubt, stuff like this happens."

Joy explained to her that God was allowing these things to surface so that she could see that her heart needed to heal, because if she continued, she would push him away.

Joy encouraged Kay to seek counseling. Kay informed her that she and David had already agreed to set up an appointment with

Pastor Richardson. Joy breathed a sigh of relief because David had confided in Joy that he was thinking of taking their relationship to the next level. She changed the subject and inquired of Kay's relationship with her mom. Kay was very excited to tell Joy that things could not be better between her and her mom, although she felt that her mom could be overly protective at times, but they are at a great place. They were deep in conversation until Joy looked at the clock and realized that it was over an hour since David and the girls had left.

Where did the time go? David and the girls should have been back by now. Just as Joy was about to call the boutique, there was a knock on the door, and Jazz came in.

"Where are the others? Joy asked.

"Oh, they had to make a stop, but they're coming soon," Jazz responded. Coming to sit by Joy on the sofa, Jazz said to her mom, "Mom, Dad said to call him." Joy pretended not to hear her by inquiring why the others had not returned yet. Jazz was not about to give up so easily. "Mom, did you hear me?" she asked.

"Girl, you and your father should leave me alone," Joy said as she got up and went to her room. She told Jazz that she was going to lay down for a while, but she should call her when the others got back.

Jazz looked disheartened. "Mom, what if it's important?" she asked.

Joy did not respond but went in her room and shut the door.

Kaylynn looked at her friend, thinking how wonderful it would be to have a father around. She could only imagine how Jazz felt. She knew that Jazz was mad at her dad for breaking up the family and would not speak to him at first. "Have you changed your mind about your dad now?" Kay asked Jazz.

"Hey, God moves in mysterious ways, His wonders to perform, you just never know. But one thing I do know is that they still love each other. I know my dad didn't leave any mysterious papers here. He just uses it as an opportunity to call Mom. But the funniest thing about it is that I think Mom knows. However, to answer your question, I'll be okay with whatever God does," Jazz said.

"So if you'll be okay with what God does, why wouldn't you give Jah'Vaughn a chance? God moves in mysterious ways, that's what you said." Kay knew she was treading dangerously but decided to anyway. "All he's asking is to take you out to dinner. What harm is in that?" she continued.

Jazz looked at her for a moment before answering. "So because it's just dinner, I should go? Do I have to go out with every guy that wants to take me out to dinner?"

"Hey, hey, hey, whatever it is, I didn't do it. What is going on here? If you hate the idea of going out with Jah'Vaughn that much, I promise I will not bring it up again," Kay said, feeling a bit hurt. But Jazz saw the hurt on Kay's face, and she apologized, explaining to her that it was not about Jah'Vaughn but something that had been bothering her for a while. As soon as Jazz decided to tell Kay about it, there was a knock on the door, and she realized that this was not the right time. She promised Kay that she would talk to her when the time was right.

Another hour had passed before David and the girls finally return. "What took you all so long?" Kay asked.

"Why don't you ask your boo?" Cassie replied. "Men usually know what they want, but he had to be picking and choosing. I told Lisa, 'Let's go, he can find his way,' but she is so nosey, she wanted to wait for him."

"Mom," Kay said, "you wanted to leave him? You know he is new to this area and will get lost."

"Girl, I only said that so he would hurry up," Cassie replied as she went in the bedroom to get Joy. They were about to surprise Kay for her birthday. She had already told them she did not want a party, but Cassie always had to have things her way and decided to have a party anyway.

They all gathered around and sang happy birthday to Kaylynn. Cassie hugged her daughter, thanking God for granting her another year and complimenting her on her success in achieving her doctorate in psychology. When it was David's turn, he wished her happy birthday again, and then he took her hand, and as he pushed his hands into his pocket, they all started screaming so loudly that they did not even hear when he proposed. Kay was so nervous that her hands were shaking, and it took David a minute to get the ring on her finger. The rest of the night seemed like a blur as they all took turns in looking at the ring. Jazz was so happy for her friend that, for a while, she forgot about her own situation. As the night ended, everyone was already talking about wedding plans, and Joy was already thinking about the menu.

Chapter 10

It was a week since the birthday/engagement party for Kaylynn. She still could not believe that she was planning her wedding. She thought about what colors she wanted to use but kept changing her mind from one minute to the next. Her mom told her that she would drive herself crazy if she didn't relax, but trying to convince her that everything would be okay was going through one ear and out the next. Today was no different. Here she was, covering for Lisa at the boutique, but she could hardly keep her mind on what she was doing. She had yet to ask Jazz to be her maid of honor, although she would think that Jazz should know that by now. Just as the thought crossed her mind, Jazz came through the door.

"What are you doing here, and where is Auntie Lisa?" Jazz asked.

"Do I need a reason to visit my best friend?" Kay replied. She continued to explain to Jazz that she came to see her, but Lisa had to step out for a minute and had asked her to cover for her. Jazz took Kay's hand to look at the ring for the tenth time since last week. Kay's smile warmed her heart. She could feel the joy that was oozing from her. She hugged her best friend as Kay asked her to be her maid of honor. Jazz said yes, and they began to discuss the plans for the wedding. She wanted to know if they had picked a date already. Kay told her that she and David had agreed on October or November of next year, which would give them a year to plan properly, to which Jazz agreed.

Since they were alone, Kay took the opportunity to ask Jazz about what had been bothering her. As soon as Jazz began to share with her friend, a customer walked in.

"How soon do you have to leave?" Jazz asked her.

Kay looked at her watch. It was only 11:45 a.m. She told Jazz that she had to meet her mom for lunch around 1:00 p.m., which would give them enough time to talk after Jazz was finished with the customer. As Jazz was helping the customer, she was praying that he would make haste so she could have that conversation with Kay. She heard the door open again and breathed a sigh of frustration. Would she ever get the opportunity to talk to Kay, she wondered.

"Good afternoon," a voice greeted Kay.

"Good afternoon, and how may I help you?" she asked.

"I'm here to see Jazmine. Is she here?" The person asked. He extended his hands and apologized. "I'm sorry. Hi, my name is Jah'Vaughn. Is she around?"

Laughing, Kaylynn said, "*The* Jah'Vaughn? I can't wait to see this. Hi, I'm Kaylynn, her best friend. She is with a customer right now, but you can wait if you like. Are you a long-time friend of hers? I've heard some very interesting things about you." Kay was rambling on, and she knew it.

"I hope it's all good things," he said. "I met her through a mutual friend, Miss Cassie. I'm not sure if you know her."

"Boy, stop tripping. That's my mom and you know it."

They talked for a while, and Jah'Vaughn told Kaylynn how he met Cassie at church through his uncle, Donovan Taylor, choir director at church. Kaylynn's eyes popped open as she started to laugh. He wondered what she was laughing at and asked her. Her only response was, "Interesting, very interesting," so he decided to leave it alone. He shared with her his enthusiasm for youth ministry and how he loved working with his uncle in the different youth programs. Kaylynn noticed that he kept glancing in Jazz's direction.

After ten minutes or so, Jazz was done with the customer and began walking toward them. As she got closer and realized it was Jah'Vaughn, she instantly became annoyed. Kay noticed the look on her friend's face and whispered to her, "You better not. I'll be in the office if you need me." Jazz ignored her. Kay said goodbye to Jah'Vaughn and went into the office. She pulled the chair close to the door so she could eavesdrop.

"Hello, good afternoon," Jazz greeted him. "How can I help you?"

"Good afternoon. How are you?" he asked.

This annoyed her more. "Again, I ask, how may I help you?"

Jah'Vaughn tried his best not to let her get the best of him. "You can help me by going out to dinner with me," he said.

She responded with such hostility. "Why did you come all the way down here to aggravate me? Get this through your thick skull. I'm not nor ever will be interested in going out with you. Listen, I'm busy, and I must get back to work. Goodbye."

Jah'Vaughn wished the ground would open up and swallow him. He said goodbye to Kay, who was just coming from the office.

She heard it all and couldn't wait to give Jazz a piece of her mind. As she came from the office, she confronted Jazz. "You did that because what? That was nasty, Jazz, and so not like you. I know you have a lot on your mind, but you had no right to treat him like that. Even if you don't want to go out with him, you could have said it better."

"I know," Jazz responded, "but now is just not the right time. If I take back what I said, he might take it the wrong way, and I don't want him thinking that I like him. Will you apologize to him for me?"

Laughing as usual, Kay replied, "Me, apologize for you? There is a lot I will do for you, but this is not one of them. You make your bed, you lay in it. Listen, he is a nice young man and he loves the Lord. It's just dinner, girl. It's not going to kill you."

"Yeah, but it can come back to kick me in the butt'," Jazz replied.

"And it won't hurt you the way you hurt his feelings a while ago. Listen, all you have to do is to make sure he knows that it's just dinner."

"Okay, I'll think about it," Jazz agreed. "Gosh," she said, "I feel like I just walked into the lion's den."

"I sure didn't hear Daniel complain," Kay replied. "God works in mysterious ways, remember? He promised that He will never leave us nor forsake us. Girl don't let me start preaching up in here. I feel a praise coming on, hallelujah."

Jazz was bubbling with laughter. "Girl, look at you, acting like a first lady. I know David is so proud of you. How are the counseling sessions going?" Jazz asked

"Oh, they're going great," Kay said. "I am so glad we decided to get counseling. I have learned a lot, and I thank God for David. He is very patient with me. I realized that I'm not as insecure as I was, and I'm learning to trust God more. See, my expectation is of God, and that makes all the difference."

Kay realized that she had not heard Jazz laugh in a while and thought that this would be a good time for them to talk about what has been bothering her. "You seem happier than I've seen you in a while. That's the Jazz I knew. Always bubbly and optimistic. What happened to her? Where is she?"

A sadness swept across Jazz's face as she responded, "I don't know. She is lost, and I can't seem to find her. She is angry, hurt, and very disappointed, and I don't know what to do about it. Oh, Kay, what I must tell you could do so much damage. It can destroy friendships and break relationships."

Kay looked at Jazz, realizing that this could not be easy for her. She hugged her, letting her know that she'd be here for her. "You're scaring me. What could be so bad that could have you confused, hurting, and angry that you can't talk to me about?"

"You are the one person that I can talk to about this," Jazz said. "It's just that talking about it means that I must deal with it, and dealing with it means that I must face some consequences. The thing is…am I ready for this?"

"You can tell me," Kay said to her, "and let us deal with the consequences together. That's what friends are for. I'm here. Whatever the consequences, I'm not going anywhere, I promise."

Jazz took a deep sigh as she said to Kay, "It's Uncle Greg. He wouldn't leave me alone. One day, he came to the boutique to see Auntie Lisa. I told him that she was not there, and he said that's a good thing. I asked him what he meant by that. He told me that he was wishing that Auntie Lisa would not be there so we could talk. I began to feel uncomfortable. But then, I realized that I may be wrong, so I listened to what he had to say, but, girl, you would not believe the next thing that came out of his mouth. I was so appalled."

"Please tell me it's not what I think it is," Kay said.

"Kay," Jazz continued, "this man looked me in the eye and told me that has been watching me and how I've grown into a fine young woman and he is attracted to me."

At that moment, Kay felt like she could not breathe, it was like time stood still. "What in God's name are you talking about? Are you serious? Tell me you spat in his face. Please tell me you did."

Kay was very furious, but before she could say anything else, Jazz continued. "Wait, wait, wait. You haven't heard the rest of it. Then he went on to say he knows that I have feelings for him also. I asked him how he came to that conclusion, and he said he just knows. He then leaned over the counter and tried to kiss me. That's when I slapped him so hard across his face and asked him to leave. The thing is, Kay, I have been blaming myself. Maybe I did something to cause it. I don't know. This is Uncle Greg, Kay. I was so hurt. And to think that Auntie Lisa is seriously thinking of giving him a second chance."

Kaylynn spun around and held her head. "She is what? Are you serious? How long ago did this happen, Jazz?"

Jazz informed her that it happened about a month ago. "Remember the first time when he got back in town and came looking for Auntie Lisa at the boutique? Well, she was in the back, and I told him she was not there. When he greeted me, he hugged me and his hands lingered a bit. That made me uncomfortable. It just felt weird. Then he came back about a month ago, and that's when this happened."

"Why didn't you tell your mom?" Kay asked.

"I thought about a lot of things. First, the time just never seemed right. Second, I've heard how Auntie Lisa gets defensive when Mom and Auntie Cassie advised her to be careful. Who says that she will believe me? And that can ruin friendships."

"You have to tell your mom," Kay advised her. "You cannot keep something like that away from your mom. And it is something that Lisa should know about. It must be dealt with. Please don't put it off any longer."

Jazz breathed a sigh of relief. "Thank you so much for being there. I feel better already. Oh my goodness, look at the time. Your mom will kill you if you miss your lunch date with her. By the way, please don't say anything to her. I must speak with my mom first. You know Auntie Cassie. She is your mom. Do I make myself clear? You both have other things to discuss. Look at you. I can't believe that you're getting married soon."

Kay had a mischievous grin on her face. "Oh man, that was going to be the first topic of discussion, but I hear you. I know Mom will go ballistic on Greg. She will kill him. By the way, from now on, it's Greg with a small g. Forget that crap. Uncle my foot."

"You and your mom are just alike," Jazz said with a smile.

"I'll let you know the minute I talk to mom. Anyway, enjoy your lunch."

They said their goodbyes, and Jazmine felt lighter than she did in weeks.

As soon as Lisa returned, Jazz decided to take her lunch break. She needed to get away from the boutique for a while. Being around Lisa made her a bit uneasy. She would have her lunch at the Seaside Grill, where she could sit on the outside while soaking up a bit of sunlight as she watched the world go by. Mothers were strolling with their babies, and couples came in holding hands. Some ordered take out and some ate in. She was deep in thought, wondering if life would ever happen for her. Jah'Vaughn's face came to her mind. She shook her head, trying to ignore the image that constantly plagued her. Maybe if she just went out with him once, it would disappear. It seemed like the perfect solution, and she decided to give him a call once she got home.

Lisa asked Jazz to make the bank deposit for her. She offered Jazz her car, but Jazz decided to walk. "A little walk never killed anybody. It keeps your heart healthy and your body fit. It's only ten minutes away. I heard you complaining about putting on weight the other day."

"I know," Lisa admitted, "but hurry up. I think I'm going to close early today. I'm feeling a bit under the weather."

"Okay". "I'll be right back," she said as she left for the bank.

Chapter 11

Jazz told her mom the whole sordid story about Greg's behavior toward her. Joy was furious and thought of telling Dave, but that would make a bad situation worse. Dave never liked Greg and would only tolerate him at family events for Lisa's sake. Joy couldn't understand Dave's dislike for Greg, because as far as she was concerned, it was the pot calling the kettle black. The only difference was that Dave wouldn't dare put his hands on her, but they both had no respect for the fact that they were married men.

Jazz apologized for not telling her mom sooner. "Oh, Mom, I'm sorry that I did not tell you sooner. All I kept thinking about is what this would cause between Auntie Lisa and us."

"You leave that up to me," Joy said, "and right about now, I don't care about that. But don't ever let me hear you blame yourself for what that idiot did. You did nothing to cause it. I've always known that he was up to no good, but you can't tell that to Lisa. It's almost crazy to think that she wants to give him a second chance. God have mercy on that woman."

Jazz was at the point of tears. She wondered what would happen to her job at the boutique and their friendship. *Why did this have to happen, God? Why?*

After sharing her concerns with her mom, Joy hugged her daughter and assured her that everything would be okay. "Listen to me. Remember that God is in control of our lives. I'm so mad right now, yes, I am, but I trust Him and know that He will work everything out for our good and His glory. I understand your concerns, but God has it all in control. Remember that what the enemy meant for bad, God will turn it around for good. Don't ever stop praying, trusting, and believing. As for your internship at the boutique, God's got that too. Just so you know, I called her and asked her to come over because we need to talk. I'll be here with you."

Jazz exhaled deeply. "Oh boy. How soon will she be coming over?"

As soon as Joy was about to answer her, there was a knock at the door. Joy opened the door and was surprised to see her ex standing there. He walked past her as if he still lived there.

"Hi, Dave. What are you doing here?"

He looked at her a bit annoyed. "I was in the neighborhood and decided to stop by," he said sarcastically.

Jazz ran to him, hugging him tightly. "Dad, it's so good to see you."

He looked at her and could tell that something was wrong.

"Are you sure?" Dave asked. "Because I feel like I'm about to be punished. The only thing is that I don't know what I did wrong."

Jazz continued to hold on to him as though her life depended on it. "Right now, I need my dad more than I ever did."

The telephone rang. It was Lisa calling to say that she was on her way. For a moment, both Jazz and Joy forgot about the meeting with Lisa. Dave could sense that something was wrong, but it was obvious he was not welcome.

"Oh, baby girl, I've missed you so much." He kissed her on her forehead and held on to her as tight as she held on to him.

Joy noticed how much Jazz needed her dad right now, but she had to make sure he was gone before Lisa got there. "You should have called before you came over, Dave. You don't live here anymore."

Dave was confused. "Wait a minute, wasn't it you who told me that it was okay to come by tonight? Correct me if I'm wrong. I'm sure I'm not suffering from amnesia."

Joy dropped her head in shame. "Wow, I'm sorry Dave. I forgot, and right now is not a good time. How about we reschedule for Saturday night around the same time?"

"For some reason, I feel like I'm being rushed out of here. Whatever is wrong, maybe I can help," Dave offered, but Joy knew that Lisa would be arriving soon. Jazz loosened her grip on Dave, realizing that the more she held on, the longer he would be there.

"It's okay, Dad. We'll be all right. I'll call you later. Drive safe."

Dave said goodbye and promised to be back on Saturday, as they agreed.

Lisa arrived as soon as Dave left, and Joy wondered if they saw each other. "Hey, guys, why the urgency to come over, and why do you both look so serious?" Lisa asked Jazz and Joy. For some reason she felt nervous.

Joy offered Lisa a seat and ask if she would like something to drink. Lisa said a glass of water would be fine but doubted that she would be able to drink it. The atmosphere was not very inviting, and the look on their faces made her very uncomfortable.

Joy cleared her throat as she turned to face Lisa. "Well, Jazz came to me with a complaint, but I think that you need to hear it from her. However, I want you to listen without interrupting, and then you can ask questions and say what you must, but please do us that favor and listen first."

Lisa turned to Jazz. "You're making me nervous, but I'll try my best to listen without interrupting."

Jazz tried to be courageous as she gave Lisa the whole story of what happened. "Auntie Lisa, I'm just going to get straight to the point. Uncle Greg came by the boutique about a month ago and made a pass at me. He told me that he was glad you weren't around because he wanted to let me know that he is attracted to me, and he leaned over and tried to kiss me. I slapped him and asked him to leave. But since that day, I've been feeling angry, sick, and confused. I'm sorry that I did not say anything sooner."

Lisa felt faint, as though all the blood had drained from her. "Well, well, well, and what do you expect from me? Ask you why you waited a month to tell me?"

"Auntie Lisa, because I didn't think you would believe me," Jazz replied.

The phone kept ringing, but no one made any attempt to answer it.

"And you think waiting this long would make your story more believable?" Lisa asked Jazz, but before Jazz could respond, she continued to lash out at her. "Why would Greg do such a thing when I've decided to give our marriage another chance just when we found out that we're expecting a child and he seems to be very excited? Tell me, Jazz, why would he? You are a child to Greg. I always knew that you all never wanted me to give Greg a chance, but to stoop this low is something I never expected. Thanks for showing me exactly what kind of friends you are."

Cassie used the spare key that Joy had given her to let herself in. "What is going on here? I keep calling but no one would answer the phone. I knew about the meeting, and I told Kay, 'Let's just come over.' I came over to make sure everything was all right."

"Auntie Cassie, this is not a good time," Jazz said.

"Yes, it is," replied Lisa. "Let her in. It seems like everyone else knew about this except me. And you call yourself my friend or, better yet, family? With friends like you, who need enemies?"

Joy was getting furious by the minute. "Lisa, please tell me what reason would we have for making this story up? We know that you still love Greg, and this will affect you. You are family. We've known each other since childhood. My daughter works at the boutique with you and is about to do her internship there. Come on, Lisa. What do we have to gain by doing this to you? But you know what? There is a God. He sits high and looks low, and He mingles in the affairs of men. I trust Him, and whatever happens in darkness must come to light."

Jazz held Lisa's hand. "Auntie Lisa, trust me, it's true. I would never make up a story like this. I would never do this to you. I love you, Auntie Lisa. What's my motive?"

Lisa pulled her hand away from Jazz's. "Everyone thinks they know what's best for me. I know you don't think that I should give my marriage a second chance, but it's my decision to make, and if I make a mistake, it's also my mistake to make. No one is going to dictate what I should or should not do. So to answer your question, Jazz, your motive is purely to break up Greg and I."

Jazz was beyond hurt. At this point, she was angry. "And why would I break up the relationship between you and Greg? It's not like I want him, but Lisa was ready to give as good as she got."

"Hmm, that's not what he says, but the truth will be revealed sooner or later. You, your mom, Cassie, and Kaylynn, can consider me a long-lost friend. However, I will keep my word and let you do your internship at the boutique, and your job is still available if you want it, but I'm done."

Lisa picked up her bag to leave. Jazz was crying uncontrollably. Cassie, of all persons, tried to reason with her.

"Lisa, come on. Please don't go back into that situation. Remember how he wouldn't let you work or even go back to school? He is nothing but a controlling idiot. I know ultimately it's your decision to make, but we love you and would never stoop to such a level."

Joy watched with tears in her eyes as Lisa left. How could she be so dumb? They held hands and prayed that God would protect her and keep her safe, but they knew in their hearts that no matter what happens, they will always be there for her if she ever needed them.

Chapter 12

Kay could not believe that the year had come and gone so quickly. As if it was only yesterday, she had said yes to David; now she was in Jazz's room getting ready for her wedding. Since Jazz was her maid of honor, they agreed that Kay should sleep over; that way, they could take care of any last-minute details.

"Today is my wedding day, and I can't believe that Auntie Lisa will not be here to celebrate this day with me."

Jazz looked at her in disbelief. "Are you serious? We have to be at the church in a couple of hours. We still need to get your hair done and pick up your bouquet, so why are you sitting here worrying about Lisa?"

Kay tried hard to hide the tears that were getting ready to fall. "We sent her an invitation. The least she could have done was respond."

"Did it say plus one?" Jazz asked, not expecting Kay to answer. "If it didn't, you know that's a problem right there."

Kay chuckled as she replied, "You know, I never thought about that. Did she really expect it to say plus one? If she did, then she's crazier than I thought. All I know is that, by the end of the day, I'll be Mrs. David Whitfield."

They spent the rest of the time reminiscing about their lives. Six years ago, they were at such different places. They were in high school, Kay and her mom were not speaking, and Jazz was dealing with her dad and mom getting a divorce. They could not imagine their lives being where it is today, and that they would have accomplished this much. Kaylynn earned her Doctorate in Psychology. She plans to open her own practice soon. Jazmine graduated with her Master's in Business Administration and her Bachelor's in Fashion Design and Marketing.

Kay was thinking about the times she didn't think she would make it. 'Look what the Lord has done," she said.

"And He isn't finished yet," Jazz said. "The best is yet to come. Oh by the way, I've been meaning to tell you this. Remember last year when Jah'Vaughn came to the boutique asking me to go out with him? Well, eventually, I thought about everything you said to me, and we did go out. I just never had the chance to tell you."

Kay looked at her and rolled her eyes. "No, you never did. After a whole year, I know there is more to it. Give me all the juicy details, and don't you leave anything out."

By this time, Jazz was laughing so hard. "What juicy details? Well, we went out a few times to dinner and a movie. We had fun, but that's it" The look Kay gave her she knew not to play. "Okay, soon-to-be Mrs. Whitfield, but promise me you're not going to make a big deal about this. We have decided to be good friends, so we call each other every so often just to touch base and go out sometimes. I told him not to push the issue and not to pressure me, and he agreed."

"See," Kay said, "it didn't kill you. But do you think there is a possibility that it could develop into something else?"

Jazz took a while before she responded. "Not you too. See, this is why I didn't want to say anything. Me and Jah'Vaughn have become very good friends I don't want to mess it up. Listen, God will send me my husband when the time is right. In the meantime, I'll worship while I wait."

"Amen," Kay said. "I hear you, honey. But I know that he has strong feelings for you, and don't you roll your eyes at me. You are just trying to ignore the obvious. Everyone can see that except you, or maybe you do but you don't want to admit it."

Jazz was getting a bit annoyed. "Even if that is true, and it isn't because you don't know what you're talking about, after all the times that we have gone out over the past year and have been calling each other, don't you think I would have picked up on it by now?"

Kay decided to end the conversation. "Okay, I rest my case. However, time will tell. And speaking of time, we need to hurry up and get dressed."

Joy could hear the girls laughing as she entered their room. "Ladies, hurry up. We have to be at the church in an hour. Don't forget we have to make a stop. I'm going to get dress now, but as soon as I'm finished dressing, we have to leave." Joy left, closing the door behind her.

Dave and Cassie had come over since they were all riding in the limo with the bride. Cassie thanked Dave and Joy for being there for Kaylynn. Dave's response made her teary eyed.

"I will do anything for family, and you guys are like family to me. You and Kay have been a part of our lives from day one. We have had our differences, especially when Joy and I got divorced, but that never stopped us from being friends. So on this day, I am very pleased to stand by your daughter and do the honors of giving her away like I would my own daughter."

"Aww, thank you," Cassie said. "I don't know what I would do without you all. I've been meaning to ask you, how are things looking for you and Joy?"

Dave shrugged his shoulders. "I honestly don't know. I know for sure I want my family back. I've made some dumb mistakes in my life, but I must say this was the worst of all. I have apologized to both Joy and Jazz, but Joy is a tough nut to crack. She seems so hostile at times."

Cassie frowned, knowing all that he had put Joy through. "Have you told her how you feel?"

"She is not making it easy to have a conversation," Dave replied, "but I'll tell you this, I know she knows how I feel and knows exactly what I want. It's okay, because I'm not going anywhere."

Dave and Cassie did not hear Joy come into the living room. "What are you two whispering about?" Joy asked. "Cassie, what trouble are you stirring up over there?"

Cassie tried to hide the smile on her face. "Why would you assume that I'm stirring up trouble? All I'm doing is having a serious conversation with my brother."

Joy was looking beautiful, and Dave could not take his eyes off her. *What was I thinking of when I left this woman?* he thought. She had moved on with her life and was doing great as a businesswoman. She went back to school and completed her education, built one of the most successful catering businesses in the downtown Atlanta area, and is a professor at one of the major universities, teaching culinary arts. *I am so proud of her. Stupid, stupid me.*

Kay entered the living room looking as beautiful as ever in her Chanel lace wedding gown. Jazz followed Kay and fitted the veil on her head. As she turned to face the others, tears ran down her cheeks.

"No, no, no," Jazz said, "you're going to mess up your makeup, and we can't have that."

The telephone rang. It was the limo driver calling to say that he would be there in five minutes.

"I'm so nervous," Kay said.

Cassie held her daughter's hand and squeezed it tightly. "Hey, baby, you're going to be okay. Everything will be perfect just as we asked God for it to be."

The phone rang again; it was the limo driver. He was outside. It was time. Joy and Cassie looked around the living room to make sure they did not forget anything as they all left for the church.

They stopped at the boutique and got the bouquet and the gift that Kaylynn had ordered for David. She could not wait to see her husband's face when he open his gift. She thought about being a wife and hoped that, by the grace of God, she would be the virtuous woman he so deserved. She was so deep in thought that she did not realized when they pulled up in front of the church. She took a deep breath and looked at Jazz.

"Thank you, Jazz, for everything you've done and for always being there and for being the sister that I've always wanted."

Jazz smiled. "Thank you, my sister. Are you ready?"

"As ready as I'll ever be," Kay said.

The congregation stood as Kay and Dave walked down the aisle. Many of her friends from school were there to celebrate this day with her. She saw a glimpse of her grandmother. She did not know that her mom had invited her. She had forgiven her over the years, but they had not seen each other in a while and did not keep in touch. It was her day, and she would not let anything spoil it. As she continued her walk, she could see David looking handsome as ever standing at the altar, and everything that seemed to occupy her thoughts vanished away. The ceremony was beautiful. As they said their vows and exchanged rings, there were a lot of ooh's and ah's. But when, for the first time, Pastor Richardson presented to the congregation Mr. and Mrs. David Whitfield, the church exploded with a thunderous applause.

The day had come and gone. David and Kay left for their honeymoon. Jazz was missing her best friend and couldn't wait for Kay to return. She had so much to tell her. Cassie and Donovan seemed to be an item, her dad had been coming around a lot, and Auntie Lisa… Well, that was the biggest of all. Or maybe not.

Epilogue

It was the day before Thanksgiving. David and Kay had returned from their honeymoon. Jazz was sitting at the dining room table, staring endlessly at the clock. Her mom had made her promise not to call Kay before noon.

"Can you wait until noon?" Joy had said. "Kay is a married woman now, and you need to remember that. Look, Jazz, I know you two have been friends since kindergarten, but the rules of the game have changed. You're not going to be calling her late at nights either."

It was 11:30 a.m. What difference would half an hour make? But as soon as she picked up her phone to dial Kay, as if on cue, Joy came around the corner.

"Jazmine Sophia Brown, don't you dare!" her mom said.

Jazz laughed so hard the tears rolled down her face. "You know, Mom," she said, "I've always wondered how you do that. Do you have eyes in the back of your head or something?"

Joy could not help laughing herself. "It's called being a mom. When you have kids, you'll understand."

Jazz felt her phone buzz; it was a text from Kay letting her know that she would be calling her in a minute, which Kay did. Jazz asked her mom to excuse her and went to her room. They spoke for a while, but Jazz told Kay that she would have to fill her in the following day when they all met at Joy's for thanksgiving.

As soon as Thanksgiving dinner was over, David, Dave, Jah'Vaughn, and Donovan went into the den to watch the game. Jazz and Kay went into Jazz's room. Joy and Cassie were in the kitchen cleaning up but could hear the giggles coming from the girls in the room. Joy knew that Jazz was sharing all the juicy gossip with Kay, especially about her and Jah'Vaughn. Jazz had decided to give him a chance and continue to trust God in the process. Joy smiled as she saw Dave watching her.

"I can't believe that I'm actually thinking of giving this man another chance," Joy said.

Cassie looked at her friend with a wide grin. "And I can't believe that God has blessed me with a man after His own heart. I wish Lisa was here."

Joy looked puzzled. *Lisa and Cassie?* But she did not say anything.

The game was over. It was a long day, and they were all tired. As they were getting ready to leave, there was a knock on the door. Joy opened the door only to see Lisa standing there as if afraid to even speak. Joy knew Lisa had done wrong, but because of the woman of God that Joy was, she invited Lisa in. Everyone watched in amazement as Lisa stood there with tears streaming down her face. She had rehearsed this over and over, but standing here now, in front of everyone, she tried to speak, but nothing seemed to be happening. However for them, she didn't need to say anything. Coming here was already humbling enough for her, so they all huddled around her and embraced her. This made her cry more. She knew she had to say something. They could not just pick up where they left off as though nothing had happened. She had hurt them badly and needed to apologize.

Lisa cleared her throat and tried again. "First, I want to say thanks for opening your door and allowing me to come in after all that has happened. I came to apologize for my attitude and behavior when Joy and Jazz spoke with me that day. I couldn't believe what I was hearing because it contradicted everything that Greg told me. I was ashamed and felt stupid for believing him before I found out the truth. Please forgive me. You guys have been there for me from day one, but I could not believe that I allowed this man who had misused and abused me to make a fool of me again. I thought you would not want to speak to me after that, so I stayed away, but what touched my heart was when I got the wedding invitation. Kay, you were a beautiful bride. Yes, I was there sitting in the back of the church, but I left soon after the ceremony. I am so sorry that you missed my daughter's birth. Greg is no longer around. We got divorced, but God has blessed me with a beautiful daughter. Joy and Cassie, I can't wait for you to meet her. I thank God for you all—my family. If you would have me, I'd be happy to be back."

One by one, they hugged her again. When it was Dave's turn, he just couldn't leave well enough alone. "I'm glad you came to your senses."

Lisa looked at Dave and shook her head. "Same old Dave," she said as she hugged him.

Lisa had invited them all to her daughter's christening. They were the only family she had besides her sister. She had asked Joy and Dave to be godparents, to which they graciously accepted. After the service, they all gathered at Joy's place for lunch. David and Kay announced that they were having a baby, and excitement filled the place. Everyone was talking at the same time. Dave interrupted them by asking for their attention. He held Joy's hand as he went down on his knees and asked her to be his wife again. She said yes, smiling as he placed the ring on her finger. Donovan came and stood beside Cassie and held her hand. As if on cue, Jah'Vaughn did the same thing. He held on to Jazz as she shed tears of Joy. It felt so good to have her family back. Lisa was happy for her friends. She couldn't wait to help Joy with her wedding plans. There was so much to talk about. She held little Angel Joy in her arms, thanking God for her and for everyone here tonight. The place was filled with laughter and happiness. Lisa had not felt such joy and peace in a long time. That's what love is all about.

About the Author

Lydia Eudovique was born on the Caribbean, in the island of St. Lucia. At the age of thirteen, she migrated to St, Croix, Virgin Islands, where she finished high school, got married, and had five beautiful children. After leaving the Virgin Islands, she then moved to Florida, where she had her last son. As a child, she would spend all her spare time reading. She loved to read and would always picture herself writing one day. She enjoyed the places that she would visit while reading. Even as a child, she preferred books without illustrations or pictures. Because of her creative mind, Lydia is a now an accomplished poet, songwriter, and playwright. She has a passion for young people and wants to make a difference in their lives by giving them an opportunity to live their dreams and be the best that they can be. Because of that, she became the founder of Dreaming Big Foundation.

CPSIA information can be obtained
at www.ICGtesting.com
Printed in the USA
BVHW071637100821
614090BV00007B/289